Table of Contents

Chapter One: Introduction

Alan's Story

The warm glow of the TV was Alan's safe place. As he played video games, all his worries and troubles seemed to vanish. He was whisked away to another universe—an alternate reality where the stress of life's responsibilities ceased to exist. While there, he forgot about the people that bullied him earlier in the day, the homework that was due tomorrow, and the expectations of his parents. All of his shortcomings and insecurities were temporarily placed in a cabinet somewhere in the back of his mind. If it weren't for escapes like television and video games, Alan wouldn't know how to cope with the stress of everyday life.

Alan was an awkward kid with very poor social skills. He was not strong or coordinated, and he was self-conscious about everything he did and said. He was teased a lot, which only damaged his confidence even more. He wanted to make friends but didn't really know how. His parents were emotionally distant and didn't have great social skills themselves, so they never taught Alan how to develop a healthy social life. It was always easier for Alan to stay home and sit in front of the television playing games and living in a fantasy world.

Initially, Alan's parents didn't really mind that he played a lot of video games. Playing seemed to make him happy and keep him occupied, which allowed his parents to have some time for themselves. As long as he got his homework done and wasn't disrespectful, his parents didn't see any reason to push him to play less often. As time passed, however, the games that Alan was playing got more immersive and sophisticated. He started to spend even more time playing them and his grades started to suffer. He began procrastinating worse than he ever had, which led to lots of fights at home.

These fights would sometimes get so bad that Alan's parents took his video games away. When this happened, Alan became extremely sad and sometimes enraged. He felt empty and retreated into his own world. Sometimes, he would just lie in bed and look at the ceiling. Other times, he might read a book or engage in some other hobby, but he never seemed to enjoy it as much. When he got the video games back, he would quickly resume playing them just as often, and the cycle would repeat.

As Alan got older, his parents began to give up trying to control his gaming. They were too afraid to take his video games away completely because of how depressed and angry he would get, but they were also too concerned to keep quiet about it. The result was an endless cycle of nagging, Alan responding with anger and defiance, and everyone throwing their hands up having accomplished nothing. Alan's grades continued to suffer and his family began to worry about him more and more.

Alan started playing online games around this time, which brought his addiction to a new level. He would spend all day in his room talking on a headset while playing games with friends from school or random people on the internet. His obsession with gaming became so severe that he would lash out at his parents if they did so much as ask him to come to dinner while he was playing. His parents hoped that Alan would grow out of this phase or simply become motivated to be an adult after he graduated high school.

When Alan did graduate high school, his parents were again let down when they realized that he had practically no motivation to work or further his education. He agreed to take some classes at a local community college to appease his parents and he began working part time to pay for his games. This bare minimum effort gave his parents some hope to hold on to, but it seemed that he would do nothing but play games all day if given the option. His parents didn't know what to do. They were too afraid to push him to move out because of how severely he lacked the basic skills to survive in the world. They felt trapped. If they allowed this cycle to continue, Alan would never grow up; if they forced him to stop, he would become depressed, enraged, and possibly harm himself. They had run out of options, and Alan had run out of the power or willingness to change.

Alan's story is one of many similar stories that are occurring in households all over the world today. Children are becoming overly dependent on video games as a means of relaxing, socializing, and escaping, resulting in an addiction that impacts every area of their lives and the lives of their family members. I often get calls from concerned parents who just don't understand why their children seem to be only interested in video games or why their adult children seem to have no interest in launching into the real world and creating a life for themselves.

This book is not an attempt to demonize video games. I grew up with video games and have a personal affinity for them. On top of that, I believe that video games do have a lot to offer. They can be an incredibly enjoyable way to spend time with friends, relax, and even learn. Due to that fact, only a small portion of this book is going to address video games themselves. This book is primarily about the *relationship* that some children (adults, too, but that's another book) have developed with video games, particularly when it's a difficult-to-control, dysfunctional relationship in which time spent playing video games is highly out of balance and causing damage to the child's life.

This book is not going to teach you how to perform miracles. It is not likely that you'll be able to convince your child to willingly and happily give up his favorite pastime. Nor is it likely that you'll be able to provide him with the skills to self-monitor and use video games in a healthy way, at least not quickly or easily. You are probably going to have to get your hands dirty. You're going to need to set limits and boundaries. You're going to need to talk openly and honestly with your child and do your best to be loving and accepting while still being firm and in control. It won't be easy, but it may save your child a lot of pain and frustration in the future.

A Few Words on Addiction

While the concept may seem simple, addiction is pretty difficult to define. The inability to stop doing something exists on a wide spectrum. One person might struggle with eating too much, while another person can't get through their day without snorting cocaine. For the purposes of this book, I will define video game addiction as continuing to engage in the use of video games despite clear consequences. The consequences may be natural consequences or consequences that have been imposed by you or other authority figures.

You can benefit from this book regardless of where your child falls on the addiction spectrum. If your child is playing video games too much and spending less time with friends, this book is for you. If your child is spending all day in a dark basement playing games and refusing to shower or eat, this book is for you as well. Basically, if you have a child who is playing too many video games and doesn't seem to be able to stop on his own despite consequences, you've come to the right place.

What is Video Game Addiction?

While most people can probably play video games without letting things get too far, there are some who can't. For reasons that we have yet to fully understand, the pleasure-reward center of some individuals' brains are easier to hijack. Activities that would bring a moderate amount of pleasure to some bring significantly more to people we would identify as "addicts." The old-fashioned belief was that these individuals lacked the willpower to snap out of their addiction and get their lives together. We now have increasing evidence to suggest that the situation is more complex.

According to a body of research conducted by Dr. Roy Baumesiter, our willpower appears to be a finite resource[ii]. My personal and professional experience has led me to believe that people who become addicted often don't lack willpower and actually have very strong wills when it comes to other areas of their lives. I argue that the problem with all addictions, including video game addiction, is not a lack of willpower, but a level of craving that quickly depletes one's willpower, no matter how much they may have.

Children are more prone to this addiction for a few reasons. First, their brains are still developing, and they will be until they're around 25 (22 for girls. They really *do* mature faster)[iii]. During this phase of development, children are far less capable of delaying gratification and using their higher brain functions to exercise self-discipline and adjust their behavior. This is why you'll see kids making themselves sick from eating too much Halloween candy. In early years, it's the parents' job to make sure that the child's behaviors are kept within reasonable limits. The hope is that they then learn to regulate the behaviors on their own.

Secondly, children generally have much more social pressure to play video games. This is particularly true for boys, though it's becoming more true for girls as well. A majority of children have some sort of online gaming presence. The pressure for children to begin playing video games (or to continue playing them) is significant. If a child decides to stop playing video games, he's also deciding to distance himself from certain online and real-life friends. This is not a decision you can expect a child to make easily, especially at a stage of life where social acceptance is so important to them.

Finally, most children are simply less able to identify and avoid being influenced by the techniques used by game developers to keep them hooked. As I'll get into in a later chapter, video games are fine-tuned to regularly activate the pleasure-reward center of our brains. Children don't realize this; they just experience this as having a lot of fun they don't want to stop. They are not yet at a stage of development where they can easily understand the way their brains have been essentially tinkered with. If they understood this, it would be easier for them to step back and take an objective look at their behavior. Since most of them can't yet, we have to do it for them.

Extra Help

Before I launch into the main part of this book, I want to throw out a few disclaimers. As with any intervention or potential solution to a complicated problem, this book contains no magic bullets or guarantees. It is meant to be a source of information and to provide you with a basic foundation of knowledge necessary to successfully parent a child who is struggling with video game addiction. It is my belief that following the basic outline in this book is likely to result in positive changes, but a lot of that depends on your consistency, your level of support, your child's temperament, how long your child has been addicted to video games, and several other factors.

While I hope this book helps you, I would be remiss if I didn't suggest that you also look for family therapy that includes as many family members as you deem necessary. You may wonder why I suggest family therapy instead of just individual therapy for your child. The reason is that an issue as severe and self-destructive as addiction is *never* just the child's responsibility. No human being on this planet exists in a vaccuum. We are all connected to other people that we influence and who influence us. This is especially true when it comes to families. Families are a system. Issues are rarely caused by one individual's issue. A vast majority of the time, the issues in a family are issues with the entire system.

If you look back at Alan's story, you'll recall that his parents were emotionally absent and didn't teach him a lot of social skills. I mentioned this for a reason. I have yet to work with a struggling child that lives in a home where everything is balanced and wonderful. Even if it's not as obvious as in Alan's story, there are always patterns in the family that in some way have helped contribute to what has been labeled as the main problem. Perhaps there has been a loss in the family that wasn't fully dealt with. Perhaps the child is experiencing excess stress due to watching his parents fight and argue. Perhaps the parents work so much that the child is feeling neglected and unloved, even though the parents are just trying to provide her with a good life. No matter the cause, it's always necessary to look at the entire system. I will address that to the extent I am able to in this book, but it is not a substitute for regular therapy with a trained professional. If you are reluctant to find professional help for any reason, I hope this book can help. Ideally, however, doing both gives you the greatest chance of success.

If you do decide to seek therapy, keep in mind that there are many options. You could work with a master's level clinician such as a marriage and family therapist (LMFT), a licensed professional clinical counselor (LPCC), or a licensed clinical social worker (LCSW). Alternatively, you could work with a doctorate-level clinician such as a PhD or a PsyD. Regardless of what you choose, do not be shy about asking lots of questions about them and their qualifications. Just because a clinician is licensed does not mean that she is an expert on family systems therapy. You are paying your therapist to help you and your family. You are more than entitled to make sure she can meet your needs.

A Crash Course on Intermittent Reinforcement

This concept is going to be essential to understanding several of the topics in this book. I want to introduce it here as it's going to be mentioned often. It may sound complicated, but it's a straightforward concept that everyone has experienced. Reinforcement is anything that motivates a living being to repeat something. The most classic example is telling a dog to sit and then giving it a treat when it listens. The dog learns that sitting when told is rewarded, and therefore sits when he is told. The treat is the reinforcement.

Intermittent Reinforcement is (insert drumroll here) reinforcement that is given intermittently or unpredictably. This type of reinforcement is significantly more effective at keeping a behavior going long-term[iii]. If we think about it logically, it makes a lot of sense. Let's go back to the example of giving a dog a treat for obeying a command. If you give this dog a treat every single time she obeys, she will expect a treat every time. When you stop giving her a treat every time she sits, she will quickly learn that something has changed. She will realize that she is no longer getting treats, which results in her quickly feeling less motivated to do the behavior. Now, let's imagine you were giving this dog a treat every three or four times she obeyed a command. In this scenario, when you stop providing treats, the dog will not immediately realize something has changed. It will take far more time for her to notice a change in the pattern since not getting a treat is something she's used to. It also means she *might* get a treat next time.

This works for people as well. Think about the gambling addict sitting at the slot machine believing that the next game *could* be the one where he strikes it rich. This behavior is enforced because, even though gamblers lose most of the time, they occasionally win, and there's always the possibility it will happen again. Imagine if a 50¢ slot machine gave exactly one dollar every time you played. This would be great for a while, but it would only take one or two instances of getting nothing to convince you the machine was no longer working, and thus convince you to stop playing.

This concept is important to understand for two reasons. For one, it is how some video games keep people hooked. Secondly, it contributes to how successful rules and boundaries are going to be at changing your child's behavior. If you allow your child to talk his way out of a consequence once in a while, it strongly enforces that behavior. By understanding intermittent reinforcement, you will hopefully be more aware of how big of a potential setback it may be if you give in to your child's attempts to push boundaries.

Boundaries: What They Are and What They Aren't

You'll be reading the word "boundaries" a lot in this book, so it makes sense to spend a little time explaining what they are. Boundaries are a necessary component of a healthy relationship, regardless of whether it's a relationship with a child, parent, sibling, or your mail carrier. A boundary is a limit. It is a rule that tells other people how they can behave towards you and how they can expect you to behave towards them. For example, you may be the kind of person who (wisely) refuses to loan money to friends due to the drama it can cause. That's a boundary. You are identifying a need you have (being as free from drama as possible) and setting a limit in order to make sure that need is met. In this book, you'll be hearing a lot about setting boundaries with your children. An example of a common boundary with children is not letting them speak disrespectfully to you without consequences. Parents who don't have boundaries with their children often end up manipulated, powerless, and frustrated.

Boundaries are the rules, and *setting* boundaries is the act of communicating to the other person what your boundary is. You may have a boundary, but the people in your life may not know that it's a boundary unless you tell them. When dealing with children, it is *exceptionally* important to improve your ability to effectively set boundaries. This doesn't have to be done with anger or hostility. In fact, it's best if it isn't. Boundaries need to be communicated in a way that the other person can be receptive to. This doesn't always mean the boundary will be respected, in which case further actions need to be taken. More on that later.

When I discuss setting boundaries with clients, they often get nervous because they see it as a form of conflict. While setting a boundary certainly can lead to conflict, it doesn't always have to. Boundaries are best set in a calm, loving, respectful way that doesn't involve criticizing the other person. A boundary that is set skillfully is often much easier to accept than one that is shoved down a person's throat. How you set a boundary will depend on the person with whom you're setting it. If you're setting a boundary with a good friend that is mature and respectful, it may be entirely uneventful. If you're setting a boundary with a toddler, it's probably not going to go as smoothly. You'll need to alter your approach depending on your audience, but the end result is the same: you have a limit and you need the other person to abide by it.

I'll be repeating this a few times throughout the book because it is a crucial thing to remember. Once you set a boundary, you *must* enforce that boundary consistently. One of the most damaging things you can do to a relationship is to allow your boundaries to be crossed. It's actually more damaging if you allow your boundaries to be crossed certain times but not others. For example, if you want your child to stop using electronics at 9:30 PM, you need to stick by that every night. If you occasionally let her go past 9:30, you will end up having lots of fights and power struggles. The people in your life need to know what to expect from you with consistency. Otherwise, it results in a shaky, inconsistent relationship that makes you prone to being mistreated.

Recall the earlier section on intermittent reinforcement. By applying this principle to boundaries, you can start to understand why occasionally allowing a boundary to be violated is such a detrimental thing to do. If your child cries and throws a tantrum, and you respond by doing what the child wants every 5th time, you may feel like you're doing a great job by not giving in four out of five times, but you are actually reinforcing the behavior *more* than if you were always giving in. That's pretty unfortunate, isn't it? Nevertheless, it's the way behavioral psychology works, and you can either be the victim of it, or understand it and use it to your (and your child's) advantage.

This beginner's guide to boundaries is going to be critical to remember throughout this book. If I could only teach one lesson to parents who are trying to change a child's behavior, it would be this one. There are other tips and techniques that can help, but consistent boundaries are the foundation upon which everything else is built.

Setting boundaries is hard, and sticking to them can seem even harder. Taking care of yourself and doing your own inner work is likely going to be a necessary part of successfully altering parts of your parenting style. You can't parent effectively if you aren't engaging in regular self-care. Maintaining solid boundaries with children, the world's most skilled manipulators, takes all the strength and willpower that you can muster. Make sure you're looking after your physical and mental health so you can be successful without running yourself ragged.

A Brief History of Online Gaming

Pong, the first arcade game to receive critical acclaim, was created in 1958. It was meant to be a sort of digital version of table tennis. It was later made into versions that could be played at home on personal video game consoles. Two players, each with a controller, moved a small vertical line on their respective side of the screen. The vertical line, which represented the player's paddle, could be moved up or down. In the middle of the screen was a dotted vertical line that ran from top to bottom. This represented the table tennis "net." A small white square, representing a ball (round things were very difficult to make back then), would bounce back and forth between both sides of the screen. Each player had to move their respective paddle into position to intercept the ball and bounce it back to their opponent. When the ball made it past a player's paddle, the opposing player earned a point, which was displayed as a large, blocky number on top of the screen.

That was pretty much it. Nothing terribly complicated or involved. Because it was so simple, pong wasn't a game that was easy to get hooked on. Sure, there were some people that played too much, but it ultimately had very little going for it that would keep someone compulsively coming back for more. You'd play it for a few minutes, maybe an hour, then put it down and move on to something far more interesting.

As technology advanced, video games became increasingly more complex and involved. In the late 70s and early 80s, we experienced the Golden Age of arcade games[liv]. Around this time, home gaming systems were still struggling to take off, and in 1983, sales crashed and the home gaming industry seemed doomed. Ultimately, however, this crash gave rise to companies like Nintendo and Sega, which you are likely familiar with whether you play video games or not. These companies released several wildly popular video game consoles that breathed new life into the home gaming industry and helped shape the world of video games as we know it today.

Games continued to become longer and more immersive with each subsequent advance in technology. Super Mario Bros., one of the most popular early titles, was released in 1984 for the Nintendo Entertainment System (NES). Unlike Pong, this game could potentially take a few hours to complete. This progression continued with games like Final Fantasy VII, an incredibly popular title released for the PlayStation in 1997, which could potentially take anywhere from 40-90 hours to complete. Additionally, people often played it multiple times since each playthrough had the potential to be a very different experience depending on the choices a player made. This kind of investment of time and energy increased the likelihood that a person could feel compelled to continue playing.

Computer games were the first to allow players to interact with each other via cyberspace. At first, online play was slow and often cut short due to technical problems. Regular telephone lines were required to connect to the internet and a single phone call could cut a game short. Nevertheless, online gaming became incredibly popular and software developers started making games that had more robust online features. Games began to incorporate new ways to connect players through things like voice chat and online "lounges" where players would hang out and chat casually.

With online games, there was a new level of motivation to play: social interaction. Players would often set specific times to meet with friends online so they could chat and play. The introduction of social interaction to computer gaming was arguably the most significant change in regards to how "addictive" games could be. It often led to players feeling obligated to log on in order to maintain online relationships and not abandon commitments they had made to other players. In many cases, children developed richer social lives online than in real life. Online friendships often had the potential to be more rewarding than real-life friendships.

Online gaming became so popular that developers began creating games that were meant to be played *exclusively* online, the most popular of which is a category of games known as Massively Multiplayer Online Role-Playing Games, or MMORPGs, the most well-known title bing a game called World of Warcraft. You've likely heard of this game due to its incredible popularity. It was released in 2004 and hit its peak in 2010 when it reached 12 million active players. Millions still play the game today. This particular game likely did more than any other game to shed light on just how addictive online gaming could be. It was common to hear stories of children (and adults) playing the game for 16 hour stretches or more. It represented a major milestone in game developers' abilities to create a world that kept people invested.

Today, game developers continue to search for ways to keep players hooked on their games, and why wouldn't they? Game development is an industry like any other, and creating a product that people want to use is what they're supposed to do. While it would be nice for developers to spend more time contemplating the effect their games may have on some, it's unrealistic to expect them to. The responsibility lies with us to manage our and our children's use of these products.

The Goal of This Book

This book will focus primarily on strategies for parenting children addicted to video games, whether they be games played on the computer or a console like the PS4 or Xbox One. These principles and strategies can certainly be applied to other kinds of addictions (like electronics or television) as well, but the language in this book will mostly focus on video gaming. Most likely, the type of video gaming that your child is addicted to involves some level of online interaction, so I will be mentioning the social component of video game addiction often. However, if your child is addicted to games that don't have a strong social component, that's not a big deal. These strategies can still help.

There is no one magic bullet solution for every child. Your approach to helping your child break free from his or her addiction will largely depend on your relationship with the child, the child's temperament, and how severe the addiction is. No information in any book is a substitute for your relationship with your child and your intuition as a parent. That being said, there are some very basic principles that can make a big difference in a short period of time. This book will be focusing on some universally effective strategies that will hopefully improve your ability to peel your child away from the screen with as little resistance as possible, and even more importantly, keep your child from falling back into an addiction.

If you attempt these strategies and find that they are either ineffective or that you simply can't muster the willpower to utilize them consistently (which is key), do not give up. This book is not the last house on the block. It is one resource in a vast array of potential sources of help. In certain situations, it is unwise to rely only on a single book for help. For example, if your child is severely addicted to video games *and* you have a contentious or hostile relationship with them, it may be necessary to seek family therapy. Video game addiction often occurs alongside other family issues such as divorce, transition, loss, or any number of other potential stressors. This book will not cover those. You will need to see a professional to fully resolve those issues. In fact, it may be downright impossible to successfully address a more superficial problem like video game addiction if there are major dysfunctions within the family that aren't being addressed. If you aren't sure if your family fits this description, it may be worth it to get an assessment from a local therapist.

Chapter Two:
How Games Hook Us

Not all games are created equal. As I illustrated earlier in the book, games like Pong and the original Super Mario Bros. were enjoyable, but didn't provide enough reinforcement to become as powerfully addictive as some of the games that are played today. Today, game developers utilize a plethora of tricks and techniques to keep people coming back to their games.

Ideally, you want your child to feel like you have some understanding of what is pulling her into playing video games. Few things incite rebellion more than a child being given rules and limits by a parent who "just doesn't get it." If you approach your child with no knowledge of video games or what makes them alluring, your child is less likely to take you seriously and listen to what you have to say. Not that you *have to* convince your child you understand gaming addiction before enforcing boundaries, but it can help.

The Dopamine Button

Our brains are phenomenally complex organs that we do not fully understand. We do, however, know that a specific chemical (known as a neurotransmitter) in our brain called dopamine plays an essential role in motivating us to continue engaging in a pleasurable behavior. Recent research on video game addiction has shown that when certain individuals play certain games, high levels of dopamine are released, which reinforces the behavior similarly to the way drugs and alcohol do[v]. While it may sound strange to talk about this in terms of neurochemicals and pathways, it basically boils down to this: when something feels good, our brain tells us to do it again.

This mechanism evolved for very good reasons. Before civilization as we currently know it, surviving was much more of a struggle. Our brains developed a feel-good response to certain survival-promoting actions in order to motivate us to do them repeatedly. For instance, when we eat fat, we experience it as delicious and our brain tells us to eat more. This was very useful back when food was scarce and we needed to consume as many calories as possible to survive. Fat is very high in calories, so it's wise for our brain to tell us to eat it whenever possible. Nowadays, to the detriment of our health and waistlines, food is more plentiful than it ever would have been out in the wild, and being driven towards high-calorie foods is causing more harm than it is good, hence our current obesity epidemic. In addition, food companies create foods that are specifically loaded with the stuff that releases dopamine in our brains, much like game developers do with games.

Things like social interaction and play also make us feel good (i.e. release dopamine) because they are essential for survival. We are social creatures and our survival chances increase dramatically when we are bonded with others, which we accomplish through socializing and playing. As with food, the availability of social interaction and play is much greater than it ever was back when we were evolving. We used to have to make the effort to go out into a community to socialize and bond with others, and the population of our particular tribe or village was relatively small. Now, we just need to shuffle over to the couch and turn on our computer or video game console. Within seconds, we are connected to millions of people and experiencing the rewards of play and socialization without having to exert much effort at all.

As infants and toddlers, before we discover video games, we are all naturally drawn to other people. We socialize and play with them as often as we can. This helps us learn about the world, ourselves, and how to have relationships with others. It is an essential part of growing as a human being. Our brain rewards us for doing these things so that we'll continue to do them and develop mentally and emotionally. It takes effort to do this, but we are happy to put forth that effort because the reward is worth it to us.

One day, our parents plop down an iPad (or similar electronic device) for us to play with. We learn quickly that we can experience as much, if not more, pleasure just by sitting down in front of this device and letting it beam entertainment directly into our brains. It requires less effort than talking to other children and is completely under our control. We can start, stop, or pause whatever we're doing whenever we want. We don't experience the same kind of conflict, anxiety, rejection, and frustration that we do when interacting with others who have needs, want to share our toys, and occasionally mistreat us.

Electronic devices can hold the attention of a toddler for quite a while, but it's rare to see toddlers become as powerfully addicted to them as older children do. This is likely because toddlers don't yet have the mental ability to fully comprehend what is happening with the device. They will enjoy electronics, but still find interest and joy in interacting with old-fashioned toys and people. As children get older, however, they are better able to utilize all the bells and whistles that their electronics contain. They can dive deeper into the digital world and therefore become more immersed. As their mental faculties grow and develop, they are more prone to being tapped into by electronics.

The release of dopamine in our brains used to be something that required effort. Today, developers of games, movies, food, or anything pleasurable have essentially found our "dopamine button." They have discovered reliable, consistent ways to elicit a pleasure response and have us coming back for more. What used to be an art has now become a science. Social media is a prime example of this. When you open up Facebook or Instagram, what happens when you see the notification icon lit up? You may not even notice it because it's so automatic, but it most likely causes a brief burst of pleasure. You may feel accomplished, wanted, excited, or any number of positive emotions. In addition, this experience is unpredictable. If we knew we were going to have two notifications every time we opened up Facebook, it would be far less rewarding than the feeling of being pleasantly surprised by two.

Sometimes, we log on and our notifications are lit up, and sometimes they aren't. Now that you've learned about intermittent reinforcement, you can understand why this keeps us hooked. Every time we open our social media app, we look at our notifications. Occasionally, we don't see anything, but we come back because we know there's a good chance there will eventually be something there. This constant re-checking becomes almost automatic. How many times have you opened a social media app on your phone or computer, closed it, and then opened it again a few seconds later without even thinking? It's OK, you can be honest. There's no judgment here.

Many of us have become zombies whose brains have been hijacked by various apps, games, and devices. In many cases, our habitual behavior is not damaging enough for us to really desire to change it. For some, however, the habit can become an addiction and start to cause real damage. This is especially true for children, who are particularly vulnerable to this hijacking process on account of their poor self-control and immature coping strategies. A child's dopamine button is not well-guarded.

Not every child will get the same level of pleasure from using electronics. For one reason or another, there are some who just don't seem that interested. While experts have some theories, we don't fully understand why this is. Nevertheless, it seems to be the reality. There are children out there who can play video games for a few hours (even the more addictive ones), put the controller down, and then go play a sport or spend time with friends. Many children, however, start to experience so much pleasure from electronics with so little effort that they shift from playing as a hobby to playing as a primary means of feeling good. When a child reaches this state, they will continue to play video games despite negative consequences, whether they are imposed on them by the world or by their caregivers.

How Games Press Our Dopamine Button

Game developers use several different techniques to keep people coming back to their games. There are many methods they can use, and they tend to use more than one. In this section, I'll describe some of the more powerful forms of reinforcement that game developers put into their games.

Novelty

Game developers know that new experiences do a great job of pressing our dopamine button. One particular genre of games where this is seen often is in MMORPGs (Massively Multiplayer Online Role Playing Games). The virtual worlds in which these games take place are so vast that players generally can't traverse the entire world without some special mode of transportation. Playing in a world this big gives players a seemingly endless number of new places to discover. Every new discovery comes after a period of exploring and searching for some unique location or experience. Every time the player discovers something new, there is some form of reinforcement, whether it be in-game currency, experience points, or just a notification with music and a victorious sound effect. These all release hits of dopamine that reinforce the desire to explore further.

In games such as World of Warcraft, a new player begins playing in what's called a "starting zone." Once they spend a few hours becoming more powerful, they then need to walk to the local capital city. This can sometimes take as long as 15-20 minutes. At this point, they still will have seen less than 1% of the total world. The feeling of arriving in a new virtual city after a long journey is one of the many kinds of extremely rewarding experiences an MMORG player can have thanks to the sheer size of these digital worlds. This aspect of the game pulls players back, since they are always looking for the next new experience.

Game developers know that even the most massive virtual worlds can become boring given enough time. To remedy this, they often release what are known as "expansion packs." These are essentially purchases that add an entire new experience to the game. Sometimes, it's a new type of playable character, sometimes it's a new explorable area with new quests and items, but more often, it's a little bit of everything. While I have no evidence to prove it, it seems obvious that game developers carefully plan the release of these expansion packs to occur when players start to lose interest. It's not uncommon for an expansion pack to add hundreds of hours of playable content, which tends to renew interest in the game.

As of the writing of this book, the game Fortnite is being recognized as one of the more addictive recent game releases. The developers of this game have gone one step beyond expansion packs and created "seasons" much like a season of a television show. At regular intervals, the developers release brand new content that players are highly invested in experiencing. You wouldn't swear off your favorite Netflix show just before the new season came out, would you?

Games like the mobile game Candy Crush also use novelty to keep people hooked. There are *always* more levels to play, and each level is slightly different. The game never really ends. Even if it did end, the developers of Candy Crush have released multiple versions of the game, and it's not uncommon to see devotees of the game switch back and forth between versions of it in order to keep from getting bored.

In the same category as novelty is the ability to create. Games like Minecraft, Super Mario Maker, and other "sandbox" games give players the freedom to create levels or worlds that are completely unique. One can play these games a million times and never have exactly the same experience. When a game is a novel experience every time it's played, it holds players' attention much longer and has more addictive potential. It should be said that creativity in games can be an excellent way for children to express their creative side. It isn't bad in and of itself. Like all things, however, it needs to be a balanced part of a more well-rounded life.

Social Reinforcement

The "MM" in "MMORPG" stands for "massively multiplayer." These games often have millions of active subscribers at any given time. They don't all inhabit the same world, so the worlds are split up into various "realms" or "servers." Each server has a copy of the world, and several thousand players will inhabit that particular version of it. Think about that for a moment. It used to be considered exciting to play a game with *one* other person. Now, we can log online and play a game with hundreds or thousands of others.

Not only is it likely that the player will develop relationships through the game, it's generally expected in order to succeed. For example, it is often necessary for many players (anywhere from 2-40) to get together to defeat a certain enemy or complete a certain quest. In addition, players can join teams (sometimes called "guilds") that are similar to sports teams. Players get to know other members of the guild quite well and are expected to be present in the virtual world on a regular basis. This feeling of community and obligation is a major component of what makes these games so addictive. Once relationships have been established in-game, quitting the game would mean cutting off rewarding relationships.

Some of the recent mobile game releases have players log into their Facebook account to "connect" with friends, ask them for extra lives, give them in-game gifts, etc. We naturally have a desire to do something that others are doing. If players of a game can see which friends are playing, what they scored on a given level, and how far they've progressed, it gives players a feeling of connectedness and community, which increases their level of commitment to playing.

Loot and In-Game Currency

The concept of "loot" has been around in games for quite a while. It is essentially a reward that the player obtains by accomplishing a task. This can take the form of in-game currency, experience points that enable you to make your player more powerful, armor, weapons, spells, clothing, new character looks (called "skins"), etc.

Older games had predictable rewards for given accomplishments. In Final Fantasy, one of the original role-playing video games for the Nintendo Entertainment System, enemies would "drop" a specific amount of in-game currency (which could be used to buy armor, weapons, etc.) and experience points. As new games in this series came out, game developers realized that it was more rewarding if the enemies occasionally dropped other items at random.

As we've been over a few times, intermittent reinforcement is very powerful. It's a main component of what makes gambling addictive[vi]. Once game developers realized the power of variable, unpredictable rewards, the addictiveness of games increased by orders of magnitude. In MMORPGs, one of the primary motivators in the game (especially in later stages of the game) is to get together with groups of people and repeatedly defeat certain enemies or dungeons in the hopes of getting a rare item. The act of repeatedly accomplishing the same task in the hopes of obtaining a randomly-dropped item is known in the gaming world as "farming."

MMORPG players can spend days, weeks, or even months regularly playing the same part of the game with the hope that their cherished item will be dropped by the enemy they kill. Once the item does drop, the feeling of accomplishment is profound. For some gamers, accomplishing this may feel more significant than most real-world goals they've accomplished. This experience is one of the reasons we sometimes see gamers who prefer their virtual world over the real one.

Progression

The ability to progress in games is a big motivator to continue playing. This was implemented into games relatively early as the ability to "save" a game. The player could save their progress and return to the game later. In the early days, these games could maybe keep a person playing for a few hours total. Today, there are games in which progress is practically unending, especially if the game is regularly updated and expanded. Players are stuck on a never-ending search for the next way to make their character more powerful, gain access to new areas, or partake in new activities.

In MMORPGs, for example, the level of a player's character is what allows them to access certain areas, equip certain weapons, use certain items, and fight certain enemies. Players start at level one and accomplish in-game tasks that award what are usually referred to as "experience points" or "XP." When the character gains a level he becomes stronger and gains several new perks, which is often a highly rewarding experience.

Variable Rewards and Randomness

The most addictive games tend to combine some level of predictable rewards with random rewards. As mentioned earlier, items that are "dropped" by enemies or found in treasure chests are usually random. However, that is not the only way randomness is used to hook gamers. Possibly the most popular example of randomness in a game is in the mobile game Candy Crush, which is most likely played by you or someone you know. It's a deceptively simple game that involves some skill, but is largely based on how lucky you are in regards to the puzzle pieces that are given to you at random. This combination of skill and luck makes Candy Crush and similar games wildly addictive. Every time you play, there's a chance you'll get lucky and finally beat a level you've been stuck on.

Sounds oddly similar to gambling, doesn't it? That's because it's essentially the same; it taps into the same brain circuitry. Game developers know exactly what they're doing. In addition to engineering games to be addictive, they've taken advantage of people's addictions by charging money for certain items (digital) that provide advantages in the game. These are called in-game purchases or micro-transactions, and they've made a lot of people very, very rich. In December of 2018, Candy Crush Saga brought in an average of about $1.4 million per *day* in revenue. Keep in mind that the game itself is free. All of this money is made from people purchasing digital items that help them advance more easily in the game.

Distraction

Just like with watching TV or movies, gaming can be an extraordinarily effective distraction. It feels good to get lost in a game when we are stressed. Being distracted by video games for a long period of time can sometimes lead to feelings of depression, irritability, and anxiety. When people are lost in a game, they're not thinking about their problems or processing their emotions. Unfortunately, the problems and unresolved emotions are still there in our subconscious. The longer these problems go ignored, the more stress and discomfort they cause. To make matters worse, more problems get added to the pile.

For example, let's say Linda is stressed out about her taxes being due in a few weeks. She is fairly certain that she will owe money. She's afraid to look into it and therefore avoids doing so by getting lost in video games and television. As the deadline to submit tax information approaches, Linda gets more stressed. Dealing with the problem directly would likely help her feel less stressed. However, video games and television are much quicker and easier forms of temporary relief. Three days before taxes are due, Linda turns off her video games to try and go to sleep for the night and has a panic attack.

Not only has the original stress of her taxes not gotten better, but now she has to rush and may be penalized for filing her taxes late. Avoiding the problem with video games worked in the short term, but ultimately made the situation much worse.

Obviously, video games are not solely responsible for people procrastinating. If we really want to avoid a task, we can always find something to do instead. The point is that video games are an extremely effective way of tuning out life's problems. Therefore, if someone has a lot of stress or anxiety, they are likely to be more drawn to playing video games. This is especially true if they don't have good coping skills to deal with this stress and even more true if they have trouble realizing they're stressed in the first place.

Good, Old-Fashioned Fun

While it's arguably less necessary than it used to be, game developers really do try to make their games genuinely fun. I'm not going to attempt to break down what makes a video game fun, nor would it be necessary. I just want to make it clear that video games aren't all sinister attempts at mind-control. Many of them are projects created by passionate people who want to entertain others. There are some video games that can rightly be called works of art, with stories, visuals, and characters that truly are well-crafted and highly creative.

The difference between a video game that is just plain fun versus a video game that utilizes a lot of cheap tricks to keep people hooked is that a fun video game will eventually get boring. Most things that are fun eventually become less fun over time. That's not to say we can't get addicted to fun things. There certainly are people who become obsessed with things like golf, extreme sports, hobbies, etc. The primary difference is that they are better able to cut back on that activity if they need to. It tends to look more like a healthy passion than an uncontrollable addiction.

Why This is Important

If you don't have any experience with video games, I can understand why you wouldn't care to read about them. However, I'm a firm believer that empathy is always the right place to start when challenging someone's behavior. It's crucial to understand that your child is not playing video games compulsively because he's just a lazy good-for-nothing or because he wants to irritate you. He's doing it because he's essentially under the influence of a very powerful form of entertainment that has been crafted to keep players coming back. It's not fair to expect children to be aware of this process and stop it on their own without our help.

Knowing how this process works can help in a few ways. For one, it can help you approach your child with some compassion and understanding. There's no quicker way to make your child feel resistant than to judge and criticize something that you clearly don't understand. If all they hear you saying is, "stop playing those silly games or you'll rot your brain," they are far less likely to play any active part in altering their behavior. If, on the other hand, you show them that you understand how attractive gaming can be, they're more likely to hear you out when you explain how important it is to have limits set around it.

Chapter Three: Assessing Your Child's Gaming Habit

All addictions follow the same basic pattern: there is a period of addictive behavior followed by some type of consequence which results in increased discomfort and unhappiness, and thus results in more video game playing to soothe the discomfort. To illustrate, your child's addiction to video games is a source of conflict and drama that impacts his relationship with the rest of the family. This leads to her feeling more left out and ashamed, which increases the desire to play video games as an escape.

Though all addictions follow this pattern, there are some factors such as your child's personality, the severity of his addiction, and support resources that are unique to each individual child. This chapter will help you get some clarity about your child's individual gaming habit. It will address severity, factors that increase or decrease odds of successful recovery, and what kind of resources may be available to improve your child's odds of successfully recovering from video game addiction.

Is My Child Really Addicted?

There certainly is such a thing as just really enjoying video games. The purpose of this book is not to shame anyone who plays video games or to vilify video games in general. The question, then, is how do you know if your child is addicted or if you're just overly concerned about a hobby? As I've touched on already, it's essentially about consequences and lack of control. What, in your observation, are the costs of your child playing these video games? Has it impacted relationships that your child used to have? Has it gotten in the way of academic success? Has it affected his mood significantly? What happens when you set limits? Does your child listen but act disappointed, or does he fly into a rage and seem inconsolable? Has your child promised to limit his video game use only to break those promises? Does your child neglect basic responsibilities like hygiene, brushing his teeth, and eating in order to play games? These are all important questions to ask when assessing if this is really a problem

Keep in mind that there's an important difference between video games interfering with life and video games taking the place of a hobby that *you* would prefer your child to have. For example, if your desire to limit your child's video game playing is because you think they would be great at basketball, that might be more about your expectations than an issue with your child. As parents, it's important for us to look at our potential biases against our children's interests. Gaming has often been associated with laziness and apathy. While this is understandable, be careful about rushing to judgment based on your own beliefs. This will be especially challenging for parents who grew up without video games in their lives.

In this day and age, video games are so popular that they are even played professionally. In 2015, SuperData Research estimated that the global eSports (electronic sports) industry generated around $748.8 million. The world is always changing, and it's not for me to say that gaming is an inherently good or bad way to spend one's time. It is my belief that, for some children, playing video games daily for hours can be healthy and enjoyable. I've worked with plenty of teenagers that play games for hours a day but also go outside, have a social life, do well in school, and seem relatively well-adjusted. Playing video games is not always a sign of a problem.

As I like to say often about controversial behaviors: it's only a problem if it's a problem. If your child is playing video games a lot but seems relatively happy and able to function, I wouldn't worry. If, on the other hand, your child seems "pulled" in by video games and is not functioning well in other areas of life, it might be time to talk to him and see if changes need to be made.

Severity

Addictions of all types exist on a spectrum. In the beginning days of alcoholism recovery, it was common to see people argue about what constituted a "real" alcoholic. These days, there's much more of an understanding among professionals that addiction is not black or white. Some addicts will require serious help and some will spontaneously improve for unknown reasons[vii] (but don't count on it).

This chapter will help you make an educated assessment of how severe your child's video game addiction might be if there is one at all. This will be useful when deciding the lengths to which you may need to go to get your child help. For example, if a child is moderately addicted to video games, he may be able to recover with a little boundary-setting and emotional support. A severely addicted child may require quite a bit more help, including anything from family therapy to a medication evaluation by a doctor to treat potential underlying issues such as anxiety or depression.

Use the questionnaire on the following page to help gauge the severity of your child's video game habit.

Rate the following behaviors as they relate to your child on a scale of 0-10, with 0 being the least severe and 10 being the most.

Behavior	Score
1. Your child's grades, work, or other responsibilities have suffered since playing video games.	
2. Playing video games seems to affect your child's mood.	
3. Trying to set limits on gaming causes your child to become excessively upset.	
4. Your child has not followed through on promises to change his gaming habits.	
5. Due to gaming, your child neglects self-care like personal hygiene, sleep, or eating (beyond what is appropriate for his age).	
6. When your child isn't gaming, he watches videos of people gaming or talks about gaming.	
7. Your child has lost interest in activities she used to enjoy (also a potential sign of depression).	
8. When not gaming, your child seems unhappy.	
9. Your child seems "pulled in" by video games.	
10. Other people have expressed concerns about your child's gaming habits.	
Total	

Add up your score and see where it lands on the scale from 0-100. If it's a zero, congratulations, but I'm not sure why you're holding this book. If it's 100, I'm fairly certain there's a problem. I'm not going to give you a definitive number that makes the difference between "problem" or "not a problem" because that's just not how problem behaviors or addictions work. It's entirely possible for your child to score a few points on this chart and still be a non-addicted child who simply enjoys video games. What I can say is that a higher number makes it more likely that your child is experiencing some level of gaming addiction.

While having a "score" for your child's gaming addiction may be helpful for providing clarity, I would also encourage you to trust your intuition as a parent. You know your child and you know what behavior is normal for him. If playing video games seems to have altered his mood or behavior enough to cause you some concern, then go with your gut and nip the problem in the bud. If your child has been turned into an obsessed demon as a result of video games, get honest with yourself and look into getting whatever help you can.

Impact on Functioning

Impaired functioning is one of the telltale signs that a behavior has spilled into the realm of addiction. When looking at the impact of your child's gaming habit, there are a few key areas that are important to pay special attention to.

School or Work

School (and work if your child is old enough) can be one of the first areas of functioning to go downhill when an enjoyable activity falls out of balance. The motivation to continue the addictive behavior can get to a point where it regularly outweighs any motivation to be productive. The most obvious measure of academic functioning is grades. Have they declined steeply? Have they slowly started to fall? The severity of academic difficulties is often directly related to the severity of the addiction. If addiction is severe, it's not uncommon to see grades take a drastic nose dive. If the addiction is more mild, sometimes grades end up being slightly lower than before, which can sometimes make it difficult to determine if the games are causing an issue or if your child is dealing with a different challenge. It's important to have an open, minimally judgmental conversation with your child when you notice changes like this. Avoid being accusatory and immediately assuming it's video games. Doing so can cause your child to instinctively defend her favorite pastime and shut herself off from being willing to tell the truth.

Problems with school may happen around the same time as excessive video game playing, but keep in mind that that doesn't always mean one has caused the other. If, for instance, your child is experiencing emotional issues such as depression or is stressed due to bullying or life circumstances, it could very well be possible that grades have dropped as a result of the stress and video game playing has increased as a means of coping with that stress. As I will say repeatedly throughout this book, *do not* jump to conclusions about what is causing your child's problems without first talking to him. Be curious and caring, not accusatory and judgmental. Simply stripping away video games, which may be a useful temporary coping skill, without also addressing any underlying emotional issues can make the situation worse.

Relationships

Relationships that don't center around gaming will likely start to suffer if your child is struggling with video game addiction. As with all addictions, the out-of-control behavior will always take priority over just about every other area of life. If once-meaningful friendships start to fade out of your child's life, that may be a cause for concern. Talk to your child about what is happening. Explore whether or not the change in relationships are due to anything specific that your child might be able to identify. It could easily be due to interpersonal conflict that has nothing to do with gaming. Again, don't assume.

Relationships are tough. It's difficult to negotiate with people who have different needs and wants, resolve conflict, and be considerate. It's understandable why some children (particularly ones that lack social skills or confidence) seem to gravitate more towards online relationships than real-life ones. It's a much simpler replacement for true relationships. They meet their friends online and focus on one thing and one thing only: gaming. While these relationships sometimes go a bit deeper than that, they are, for the most part, less intimate and meaningful than relationships with people out in the real world. If you notice that your child seems to be much more into his online friends than his real-life friends, it's worth talking to him about it.

Recreation

Dopamine is a chemical in the brain that plays many different roles. Most notably, it creates a feeling of pleasure that motivates us to repeat the feel-good behaviors. All pleasurable activities release dopamine in the brain. If we engage in highly-rewarding behaviors like drinking alcohol, eating rich foods, or playing video games, we keep the dopamine levels in our brain elevated. This leads to our brain adapting and expecting more. This is why we often see people's addiction progress from mild to moderate to severe. At first, a small amount of a drug or behavior is enough to make the person feel satisfied. Eventually, however, the brain changes and the original behavior isn't quite as pleasurable. This phenomenon is referred to as "developing a tolerance." This leads to the individual using more of a certain drug or engaging in more extreme versions of their addictive behavior so they can chase the original "high."

As you may be able to guess, if a person is developing a tolerance to drugs or highly rewarding behaviors, they certainly aren't going to be interested in engaging in some of the more boring activities they were interested in before. Remember that video games are *constantly* flooding your child's brain with dopamine. If your child has developed a tolerance to this, what are the chances that he is going to get excited about playing catch in the park or going on a bike ride? Unless these are activities your child is truly passionate about, I'd say the chances are slim.

Video games have been engineered to activate the pleasure and reward center of our brain remarkably effectively. It's hard for anything in the real world to compete with that level of mental stimulation. If you notice your child becoming increasingly uninterested in activities that she used to find fun and enjoyable, that is a red flag. It's important to note, however, that this is also a sign of depression. If you suspect the problem might be more severe or your child has a family history of mental illness, it's always ideal to get a thorough assessment from a professional.

Aggression and Mood Changes

Mood changes that develop due to video game addiction tend to do so during the use of video games, immediately after, or when someone is going through withdrawal from gaming (more on this later).

Todd's Story

Todd is a 9-year-old boy who I met for therapy after his parents called with concerns about his increasing levels of rage and frustration. Todd enjoyed playing soccer, spending time with his friends, riding bikes around the neighborhood, and occasionally playing video games. When a game called Fortnite came out, Todd heard all of his friends talking about how much fun it was and how he needed to start playing it. He went home and asked his parents if they could buy the game for him. His grades were not of concern and Todd was an otherwise well-adjusted child who seemed to have a variety of interests. Seeing no harm in this, his parents purchased the game for him.

For the first few days that Todd had the game, he played it for the majority of the day. His parents didn't mind too much because they understood that it was a new experience for Todd. However, after about a week of playing all day, his parents decided they needed to encourage him to take more breaks and play outside or do some more creative activities. Todd was reluctant and would sometimes complain, but he usually listened without too much of a fight.

As time went on, Todd's interest in Fortnite did not fade as it did with so many of his other toys and games. He continued playing until his parents asked him to stop. He also had started to become so engrossed in the game that he would become very frustrated when he lost, occasionally slamming his controller down. He even broke it once and had to beg his parents to buy him a replacement. Whenever his parents saw these anger outbursts, they tried to help him calm down by telling him to take a break and go do something else. This worked at times, but sometimes only made him more angry.

For Christmas, Todd wanted his parents to buy him a headset with a microphone for his video gaming console. Fortnite, like many online games these days, had a feature where it was possible to speak to the people who were playing the game with you. This allowed for more social interaction and made it easier to cooperate and strategize with others in the game. As soon as Todd got the headset, his behavior got worse.

Todd's parents would often hear him screaming into the headset when he wasn't doing well in the game or when someone on his team was playing poorly. He would sometimes throw the controller and the headset down and sob if his online friends got angry with him or made fun of him for making a mistake in the game. Although many people might expect this to dissuade Todd from playing, he actually became more attached to the game because the experience of doing well with his team was so rewarding.

Todd's parents found it challenging to control his behavior, and this only got worse when the headset was introduced. As Todd's habit progressed, his parents found it harder and harder to convince him to take breaks. He would argue more than he did before. He sometimes didn't even want to eat with the family because he was so invested in his game. One day, Todd's mother asked him to come to the dinner table. Todd didn't want to, so his mother took a firmer tone and told him to put down the controller unless he wanted to get in trouble.

Todd turned to his mom and yelled, "go away, you're bothering me!" Todd, who was usually mild-mannered and calm, was unrecognizable to his mother in this moment. He had never spoken like this before. Todd's mom described it as though he had become temporarily possessed by a demon. She was frightened and hurt by this sudden aggression. At that point, she knew something needed to change but was too afraid of his anger and wanted advice. She decided she wanted a mental health professional to talk to him, so she contacted me.

Todd's story is not at all unique. I've listened to numerous accounts from parents about how their child seems to have a different personality when playing games. The stories I hear share parallels with stories of alcoholics getting hostile when something gets in the way of their drinking. When people become too dependent on an external source of pleasure like drugs, alcohol, or video games, it's incredibly difficult for them to part with it, and they will often go to extreme lengths to protect it.

Resources

While assessing the severity of the habit itself is important, you're also going to need to take a look at the available resources that you and your child have throughout this process. Does your child have friends that she can start spending more time with? Does she have sports or activities that she used to enjoy and may be able to pick back up again? How many people live in the household that might be able to support you in setting boundaries and meeting your child's needs (such as siblings, extended family, or paid help)? Are there activities in the community that are available? Are there other fun things to do in the house? Do you have time to give your child the extra attention she'll probably need when she stops or cuts back on playing games?

In addition to resources that your child is going to need, what resources do *you* have to take care of yourself during what will likely be a challenging process? Do you have someone to confide in, like a therapist or close friend? Do you have fun and relaxing activities that you can engage in? Are you exercising, eating right, and taking basic care of yourself? Are there other parents with similar issues that you can talk to for support? As you've undoubtedly heard if you've read other self-help books, you can't take care of others if you don't take care of yourself. The process of establishing or stopping habits is stressful, especially if you're trying to change the habits of someone other than yourself. You are going to need to be your best, most consistent, most patient self throughout this adventure.

Chapter Four:
Checking In With Yourself

What you're going to attempt to do is not easy. You're trying to change something that has become habit. Changing your child's behavior almost always means changing your own behavior. In fact, it's pretty close to impossible for one member of a family to change without all the other family members changing in some respect as well. Families are a system of interconnected, complex humans. These systems tend to settle into patterns, and each member of the family gets used to these patterns, even if they aren't desirable. It can be stressful to try and change the family dynamic even if the change is for the better.

Questions to Ask Yourself

Before you begin this process, you need to check in with yourself and anyone else who is involved with parenting your child, whether it be your spouse, ex-spouse, the child's step parents, or any other authority figure. Ask yourself the following questions:

- Why am I trying to change my child's behavior? How much of it is for him and how much of it is for me?
- What am I hoping will change in my child's life as a result of this?
- What am I hoping will change in my life as a result of this?
- Is there a chance I'm bringing my own biases towards video games into this decision?
- Do I have the support necessary to stick to my guns and enforce the boundaries I set?
- Am I taking good care of myself?
- How can I minimize my stress during this time?
- Am I prepared to deal with the ups and downs of this process?
- Do I have unrealistic expectations for how quickly and smoothly this should go?
- Am I bringing my own childhood experiences, regrets, or fears into this decision?
- Am I prepared to talk openly to my child about her gaming in a way that is free of judgment and criticism?

Answer these questions honestly and openly. I'll address all of these, but it may be worth discussing some of them with a therapist or trusted mentor. The point of doing this soul-searching is to make sure that you are keeping your own personal issues out of this process. Your role in helping your child change his behavior is to be as calm, loving, and firm as you possibly can. This can't be done if you have a lot of stubborn expectations, biases, judgments or fears.

Of course you are invested in the outcome. *Of course* you want your child to thrive, but that is an emotional struggle that is ultimately your responsibility, not your child's. Your job is to set boundaries, remain firm, provide empathy, and teach your child how to be a successful human being. It is not your child's job to change so that you are no longer angry, upset, or worried. If your child feels like he needs to do this just to get you off his back, it's that much less likely that he'll be a willing participant in the process.

Getting Support

Let's face it, even if your child had absolutely no challenges and was "perfect" in every way (whatever that means), parenting would *still* be extremely difficult. You're responsible for a human who starts off with no idea how to regulate her emotions, get her needs met, or do anything but poop and eat. You do your best to teach this little one how to take care of herself while simultaneously trying to take good care of yourself and keep your life in order. Even if no other challenges were added to this scenario, it would be overwhelming.

For that reason, I think *all* parents need to have some level of emotional support. It doesn't necessarily have to be from a professional. It could be a group of friends, a parenting group, or even a parenting support forum online. The bottom line is that the phrase "it takes a village" was coined for a reason. Raising children is hard, and we need not be shy about asking for support.

The beautiful thing about having a support network is that it's extremely rare for everyone to be struggling at the same time. When you're down, others are up, and vice versa. There will be times when you reach out for help and other times when you are able to help others. A support group benefits everyone involved, and it's a shame it's so much more difficult to find them in this day and age where so much of life is digital and impersonal, but that's another discussion for another time.

I'll be honest, this is just plain harder for men than it is for women. Obviously, there are exceptions to this rule, but for the most part, men have a more difficult time being vulnerable and asking other people for help. Fortunately, that has changed a bit recently. Depending on where you live, there may be multiple fathers' groups available to check out. The website meetup.com helps people find places and times to meet with people who have similar lifestyles, interests, etc. If you search for "fathers' group" on that site, you may find something. All that is required after that is to show up at the scheduled time and location and voila! You've connected with other dads.

If you're part of a religious group or community, you've got a head start that others don't. Don't be shy about going around to members of your church who have children and asking them if they ever get together with other parents. Even if they don't seem like the type of people who open up about struggles and challenges raising children, *you* can be the one to change that. Sometimes, all it takes is one person to open up and admit that they need help for others to feel courageous enough to do the same.

If you happen to live in a rural area that isn't densely populated, you may have a harder time finding in-person groups to join. In that case, the internet is always an option. There are countless forums and websites online that are related to parenting. Find one that seems to have what you're looking for and dive right in. Post an introduction and let people know who you are. Participate in the forum by answering other people's questions and asking your own. Eventually, you will be known among the members of the forum and you will have expanded your support network.

If at any point during this process you feel so overwhelmed and stressed that you are concerned about your mental health or well-being, it is always a good idea to at least be assessed by a professional. Sometimes, we need someone who is highly trained and objective to get us through some of the more difficult challenges. Even if you have a good support group, it's often too difficult for them to give objective advice. They tend to be emotionally invested in your well-being, which influences the advice they give you. Essentially, support groups are fantastic, but if you need extra help, get it.

Setting Expectations

While I believe it's likely you will have positive outcomes if you follow the advice in this book, I would be remiss if I didn't talk about having appropriate expectations. One of the guaranteed ways to become frustrated and overwhelmed by this process is to have exceedingly high expectations. I want you to feel hopeful and to be persistent, but try as much as you can to let go of how you think this will all go. No doubt you've imagined both worst and best case scenarios at this point. The truth of the matter is that the reality will probably fall somewhere in the middle of those two extremes.

If your expectation is that you sit down with your child, talk to him about the impact gaming has had on his behavior, ask him to stop, and he responds with, "sure thing, mom/dad, thanks for looking out for me," you should probably adjust your expectations. If you expect your child to immediately run away from home and join the circus, you should probably adjust your expectations in the other direction.

Visualizing things going well is not the same as expecting them to go well. I highly suggest setting aside some time before confronting your child and visualizing a positive interaction where you speak clearly, firmly, lovingly, and set your boundaries without fear. You can visualize that while simultaneously understanding that it may not happen. If you keep an open mind to whatever comes next, you are far less likely to become hopeless or overwhelmed during this process.

A Brief Mindfulness Exercise for Expectations

It's extremely difficult to read and meditate at the same time, so I suggest reading this out loud into an audio recording device and listening to it while meditating.

Take a moment to close your eyes and sit in a comfortable position. You can sit in a chair, on the floor, or anywhere that supports you firmly but isn't so comfortable that you want to fall asleep. Once you're settled, focus on taking five or six deep breaths, concentrating on the sensation of your chest rising and falling.

Now, bring up an image of your child playing video games. Notice any emotions, thoughts, or bodily sensations that arise when you do this. Do you become tense? Nervous? Angry? Scared? Sad? Spend a minute or two focusing just on that emotion and the bodily sensation that accompanies it. You may not initially think that the feeling is showing up as a bodily sensation, but it almost always does. If you're having trouble locating it, spend a few more minutes searching for it. Many people feel their feelings in their back, throat, chest, or stomach area, but any part of your body can potentially experience a feeling related to an emotion.

Next, visualize your child *after* you've succeeded with helping her stop or moderate her video game usage. What is she doing? Is she drawing? Playing with friends? Playing an instrument? Doing her homework? Applying to Harvard? As you did before, notice any feelings or sensations that come up during this exercise. Do you get hopeful? Happy? Excited? Desperate? You may feel a deep sense of longing or wanting that is almost painful. If you do, be very aware of it, where it is in your body, and just pay attention to it and any other feelings this visualization exercise brings up. Spend a good two or three minutes focusing on the sensations and feelings and allowing them to exist. Don't judge them or try to change them. Just watch them.

Once you feel the intensity of these emotions drain away a bit, you can stop. I'd suggest practicing this regularly, or at least for a few minutes before you plan to interact with your child regarding her gaming habit. It's understandable that you would go into this with a desperate desire for it to work out flawlessly. As a parent, there is nothing more rewarding than watching your child succeed in life and be happy. That being said, the more you cling to this and feel a desperate need for it, the more likely you are to resort to old habits such as yelling, threatening, or worse to get your child to comply with your wishes. These reactive techniques may work in the short term, but they are not good long-term strategies for changing your child's behavior.

Fear

This whole ordeal is likely scary for you. Chances are that fear is the reason you haven't taken some of the steps towards addressing this problem that you know you probably should. Take a moment to think about what you're afraid of and consider the reality of those fears.

Two of the most common fears I hear from parents regarding challenging their child's gaming habit are that their child will fly into a violent rage when confronted or that they will become depressed and possibly hurt or kill themselves. I'm not going to mislead you and tell you these things are impossible, but I will tell you that these are not reasons to bury your head in the sand and not address a family problem. If anything, noticing you have these fears may help you realize that there are bigger problems your family needs to address *before* addressing your child's gaming habit.

How your child responds to this process is going to depend on a lot of factors. The one thing that trumps anything you read in this guide is your judgment as a parent and your attunement to your child's needs. If your child has previously attempted suicide, expressed suicidal intent, or shown signs of depression, it is entirely valid to be concerned that this process may trigger that. In this case, I would say it's far, *far*, more important to get family therapy, or, at the very least, therapy for your child before trying to address his gaming, which is more likely a symptom of a bigger problem than a separate problem itself. If your child seems to be in a good mood most of the time, has friends, but just gets sucked in by video games, I would be less concerned. I'll never tell any parent not to be concerned at all. Our job is to stay tuned in to the needs of our children. Concern (not to be confused with excessive worry) is a necessary part of our role as a parent.

Most children are somewhere between the two extremes I mentioned in the previous paragraph. You may have a child that seems somewhat on the cusp of depression, but has not mentioned any intent or desire to harm herself. In this instance, I would still say to seek a professional assessment first. The same goes for a child who has never been violent or aggressive before, but you have a sense that he is moving closer to engaging in that behavior. If you'd rather start this process and see how your child responds before seeking outside help, that's your decision. All I can say is to avoid trying to deal with mental health conditions like depression, excessive anger/rage, or anxiety disorders like OCD and panic without some kind of professional help or support.

I know none of this is particularly reassuring, and it's not really supposed to be. My hope is that this section has not alleviated all your fear, but has encouraged you to face it and get any help you may need. Fear is normal and gives us information about our situation. The problems come when we let our fear cripple us and keep us from moving forward in life. If you have fear about this process, use that fear to help you determine whether or not you should approach it with a professional, but don't let the fear keep you from doing anything at all.

Self-Care

I'm going to mention this at least a million times in this book. Take. Care. Of. Yourself. This means exercising, eating right, doing things you enjoy, getting enough sleep, having social support, working with a counselor if necessary, finding time for fun and leisure, and generally keeping your life as balanced and healthy as possible. I'm not saying you have to do this perfectly. Nobody does and nobody can. However, you must do your best to take care of yourself as well as you possibly can. If you aren't taking care of yourself, it is going to impact how well you're able to stay even-keeled during this process.

The process of changing your child's gaming habit is going to be a structured, gentle one. I suggest you take the same approach for improving your own self-care. I can't possibly cover the entire subject of self-care in this section. It would take an entire book (which I happen to be writing, join my newsletter at http://www.practicallysane.net to stay informed. Sorry for the shameless plug). You don't need to become the master of self-care overnight. All you need to do is take one more positive action than you did yesterday. If all you did yesterday was eat donuts and sit on the couch, today, try eating donuts, going for a short walk, and *then* sitting on the couch. None of the techniques required to improve your life are magical; they just require consistent, incremental changes.

If you're taking poor care of yourself, this is going to sabotage your parenting in two ways (at least). For one, you'll not be able to be as calm and stable as you need to be when interacting with your child. Children need to feel like the adults in charge have their stuff together and are predictable, stable people that can be relied on. If you aren't able to take consistently good care of yourself, you are going to be more reactive with your children, avoid them more, and therefore cause them to feel less secure.

Secondly, children learn by example. If they see you taking poor care of yourself, they are far more likely to do it themselves. Why should a child see any problem sitting at home playing video games all day when dad sits at home all day watching television? Why is any kid going to eat her vegetables when mom eats fast food every night for dinner? At the risk of sounding cliché, actions speak louder than words. You can tell your children to take care of themselves until you're blue in the face, but if you aren't taking care of yourself, those words will count for very little.

Biases

A bias is when a personal belief or experience skews your opinion of something either positively or negatively. Before you determine whether or not your child's relationship with video games is healthy or not, you need to look at your own relationship with them. Having a bias in any direction can potentially be problematic. If, for instance, you grew up without video games and believe they "rot the brain," you are more likely to think your child's video game use is a problem when it quite possibly isn't. If, on the other hand, you grew up loving video games and advocating for them, you are less likely to see a problem if there is one.

Take a few moments to write down your beliefs about video games. Try to get more specific than looking at whether they're "good" or "bad." Do you think they can be a positive form of entertainment? Do you think there's such a thing as a healthy gaming habit? Do you believe video games are just as valid as any other pastime? Do you think video games are the devil and do nobody any good? Be honest with yourself.

Look at your list and spend a few minutes playing devil's advocate. If you think video games literally rot the brain and have no place in the world, what evidence do you have to support that belief? If you think video games can't possibly cause any harm, how likely is that to *really* be true? Once you've looked at your biases, do your best to toss them aside and realize that what you believe about them is completely irrelevant to *your child's* relationship with them. What ultimately matters is how video games are impacting your child's life and your family's life—whether they are causing more harm than good, or vice versa.

When working with alcoholics or drug addicts, I don't spend much time talking to them about the merits and flaws of alcohol or drugs themselves. It doesn't matter. Why would it matter whether or not alcohol is "good" if it's destroying someone's life? What does cannabis' "goodness" or "badness" have anything to do with how it impacts Sally's ability to get to work on time? It doesn't. It's not worth it to put much energy into thinking about video games themselves. What matters is what your child is doing and how that behavior is impacting him.

If your child was obsessed with mustard to the point where he was too busy reading about it or tasting different mustards to focus on his schoolwork or relationships, we would say he has a mustard problem. Don't think about the object of obsession, think about the life impact of the obsession. Does your child have a video game problem, or is she able to play them in a way that may very well be healthy but makes you uncomfortable? If she was spending the same amount of time on another hobby, would it bother you as much? What if she was watching TV, reading, or playing board games? How much of your perception of this "problem" has to do with your feelings about video games, and how much has to do with a genuine impact the habit is having on your child's life. Get as honest with yourself as possible about this.

Chapter Five:
Making Your Plan

Now that you've learned a little bit about video games, what makes them addictive, what an addiction looks like, assessed your child's level of addiction, and checked in with yourself, it's time to look at what your plan of action will be. I can't stress how crucial it is to go into this with a really clear idea of what kind of words and behaviors you want to use and what kind you want to avoid. If you decide you're going to just wing it and try to talk your child out of playing video games, the chances are that you'll end up repeating your old patterns that don't work and further increasing the resistance your child has to changing.

When coming up with a plan, the first thing to determine is what you want the end result to be. Do you want your child to be completely off of video games? Do you want your child to play video games responsibly? Do you not care how much your child plays video games as long as he gets his homework done? These are all valid goals depending on what you've determined is best for your child. Still, you may need to adjust them as you move along in this process.

Moderation Vs. Abstinence

In the world of addiction treatment and recovery, moderation is often considered a dirty word. There is a longstanding idea that if someone becomes addicted to something, they will never be able to use that thing moderately or responsibly. I tend to think this is true in the majority of cases, especially for drugs, alcohol, and certain behaviors like gambling. It's very rare indeed to see a gambling addict go back to gambling once in a while and being fine with it. Generally, they need to abstain completely for lasting recovery.

Unfortunately, video games are not a simple thing. When you drink alcohol, you get drunk. Additionally, you get the *same kind* of drunk every time. There are no significantly different kinds of drunkenness depending on what you drink. If you're addicted to getting drunk, you're not going to discover one particular form of hard liquor that you can magically drink without any compulsion. Video games are quite different. If you recall the early chapters of the book, video games fall everywhere on the continuum of addictiveness. If your child is playing World of Warcraft, Call of Duty, or Fortnite all day long, he may exclusively be addicted to similar games with similar addictive qualities. If, however, your child plays just about everything addictively, it may be possible that they are so strongly pulled towards the escape of gaming that nearly any game will become problematic.

Depending on your child's age, maturity level, and consequences from gaming, I believe it is worth it to consider exploring moderation as an approach to this problem and possibly even a final goal. The initial stages of my approach involves trying to moderate use. Therefore, regardless of what your final goal is, you may still get an idea about whether or not moderation is possible. Video games may have a healthy place in your child's life. Don't be closed off to the idea, but don't be closed off to full abstinence either.

Filling the Void

Remember that you are going to be attempting to change a behavior that brings your child a lot of emotional soothing and pleasure. Take a minute to think about some of the things that you have in your life that keep you feeling sane and relaxed. Maybe you have a glass of wine at night. Maybe you watch a few of your favorite shows before bed. Maybe you have a hobby that brings you fulfillment. Whatever it is, imagine if it vanished tomorrow. How would you feel? Would it be easy for you to shift gears and do something else? It would likely be pretty tough. If you were fortunate enough to be taught healthy coping skills and have a resilient personality, you might get through it fine, but most people would get stressed out, and some might just lose their minds.

If an adult would feel stressed out losing a favorite coping skill, imagine what a child or young adult might feel. They have a small fraction of the coping skills and ability to regulate their emotions that some adults have. You may hope that your child will shrug and read a book as soon as video game time is over, but I strongly encourage you to let go of that fantasy. Something needs to fill the void that will be left when your child puts the controller down, and while you may have some ideas about what you'd like your child to do, it's probably best to do this collaboratively with your child instead. We'll discuss working *with* your child in the next chapter when we begin the process of taking your first real action.

Try to understand that, regardless of how great the alternative activities are, they will most likely not be enough to fully make up for the loss of video games. Video games have been fine-tuned to hit every dopamine button we have. Very few healthy things in the real world provide that kind of pleasure and reward. As your child spends less time gaming and more time engaging in other behaviors, she will eventually start to find more joy in the new activities. This is a natural process that occurs when quitting a highly rewarding behavior. It shares some similarities with drug or alcohol withdrawal.

Whatever you are hoping to encourage your child to do instead of playing video games, it will be more likely to stick if there is a social aspect. While I would never discount any hobby or activity that your child really seems to like, I believe it's less likely that your child will feel as fulfilled by his new activity if it is something he does alone. For example, if your child states he would like to paint or learn to draw, there's nothing inherently wrong with that, but there will be a large social component missing.

More than likely, no single thing will fill the void left by video games.

Recovery from any type of addiction generally requires a lifestyle change on a fairly large scale. With drug and alcohol addiction, what often works is encouraging the addict to dive head-first into the social aspect of recovery, such as going to 12-step meetings and spending time with other recovering addicts. Additionally, we tell addicts and alcoholics to find *multiple* activities and interests that they can use to take up their time and start releasing dopamine without the aid of a drug or addictive behavior.

You are going to want to do some research regarding different social activities your child can partake in. If your child used to be into sports, that can be an excellent replacement. It may take a little convincing at first, but it's very possible your child's passion for sports may re-emerge. If your child never really had other interests, it is still possible to find something that she will take to, though it may take a bit more trial and error. Below is an incomplete list of possible activities to suggest. It is by no means an exhaustive list, and I encourage you to be creative, but this may give you a start.

Paintball	Popular sports	Dance	Acting
Martial arts	Boy/Girl Scouts	Music lessons	Strategy board games
Art lessons	Summer camps	RC vehicles	Crafting
Weightlifting	Software programming	Photography	Working (Yes, really)
Volunteering	Writing	Cooking	Gymnastics

Regardless of what activities you think are best for your child, I again encourage you to figure this out collaboratively with him. At first, don't expect any of these to immediately spark a fire or passion in your child. Even a reluctant agreement to try one of these activities is a major success. I understand that money is a factor when it comes to giving your child the opportunity to partake in these activities. You can find some that don't require a lot of money, but you will most likely have to part with some of your hard-earned cash to provide your child with an exciting outlet that makes the separation from video games more bearable.

Planning "The Talk"

At the beginning of your intervention, you're going to have to have "the talk" with your child. This means sitting him down, expressing your concern, and going over potential solutions. There will be a lot more on this later, but in the meantime, it will benefit you to do a little planning and come up with some personal dos and don'ts for talking to your child.

Every child is unique in terms of what they respond well to and what they respond poorly to. You know your child better than anyone else, and probably better than he knows himself. I would suggest writing a list consisting of approaches that you think will work and approaches that you should avoid. For example, your child may be incredibly sensitive to criticism. In this case, write yourself a reminder to minimize any direct criticism or judgment of your child or your child's gaming habit (something you should probably do anyway).

Does your child respond well to praise? Write that on your list. Remind yourself that, during the talk, you need to go heavy on the praise and let your child know that there are many good qualities about him and things that you admire. Could your child not care less about praise? Does he prefer to just figure out what's in it for him? OK (that might make him very successful one day), approach the talk from more of a business deal standpoint. Don't waste time talking about the mushy stuff when it might work better to sell your child on the fact that he gets to choose a new activity.

Here are some more questions to ask yourself when determining what approach to take with your child:

- What is likely to upset him to the point where he no longer listens?
- What are some things I do that tend to send her into defensiveness or anger?
- What kind of interactions does he seem to respond well to, and how can I weave those into our talk?
- Does my child often feel misunderstood? How can I make sure to show extra empathy and compassion during the talk?
- Is my child more logic-based or feelings-based? Should I

appeal more to her rational brain or her emotional brain? Should I give detailed explanations or stick more to being warm and accepting?
-     Does my child prefer it when I'm straightforward, or do I need to be very gentle when I confront him?

The answer to some of the above questions is probably "it depends," and that's fine. The point is to get your gears turning regarding what kind of approach is most likely to reach your child. If you've gone to the extent of purchasing this book, chances are you've already tried things that don't work. You almost certainly have a pattern of behaviors that you do instinctively when you see your child compulsively playing games that hasn't worked well thus far. We want to avoid that at all costs. This intervention needs to feel different and meaningful. If your child sees this as just another instance of a repeating pattern, it's likely to provide the same results it always has.

Timing the talk is incredibly important. When are you going to approach your child? Are you going to march into his room, unplug his gaming system, and shout, "We're gonna talk now!"? I hope not. Knowing when to bring up a topic is almost as important as knowing how to say what you want to say. You may have the perfect talk planned and end up blowing it because your child is sick, overwhelmed, or otherwise preoccupied and not able to listen.

I'd highly suggest catching your child during a time of relatively low stress. Maybe on a weekend before he's gotten hooked into his game for the day. Recall the section in this book about how excessive gaming can lead to mood swings. When your child is in the middle of gaming, it's not much different than a drug addict in the middle of a binge. If you try and intervene at that moment, you're not going to have a great time. Of course, there's always the possibility that your child is so addicted that there never seems to be a good time. In that case, you have to work with what you have, which may involve bringing it up whenever you're able to.

It may be helpful to tell your child ahead of time that you will be wanting to talk with him. This isn't the greatest approach for children with high anxiety as it can cause them lots of it. However, if you think that prepping your child rather than dropping a bomb on him would be a better idea, that is a possibility. As with the rest of the talk, this needs to be done in a non-judgmental, calm, respectful way. You could say something like, "Hey, Arthur, your mom and I would like to talk to you a little bit later. When can you do that?" We'll get to the nuts and bolts of how to navigate the many possible responses to this in the next chapter.

Consequences

Deciding what consequences to enforce in any given situation will help you avoid reflexively dishing out punishments or making empty threats. Learning how to enforce consequences effectively is going to be a useful skill when going through this process. Consequences need to be three things to be maximally effective.

1. Predictable

2. Consistent

3. Relevant

A predictable consequence is one that doesn't surprise or shock your child. Parents sometimes like to use these as a power play or as a means of really proving a point. Don't. If you use consequences reactively, your child is going to feel bullied and overpowered, which just leads to more resistance and reactivity. Eventually, the situation escalates into a blowup. Make consequences predictable by discussing them *before* the situation occurs whenever possible. For example, if you've set up a plan of moderation with your child and told him he can't play for more than two hours in a day, he needs to know exactly what will happen if he plays for two hours and one minute. Will he lose his gaming privileges for a day? A week? Will he be required to do an extra chore around the house? Participate in another activity? You need to know, and so does your child.

Obviously, there will be situations you can't predict, in which case you'll need to make up a consequence on the fly. If this happens, it is still paramount to make sure that the consequences are not delivered in a way that is reactionary or impulsive. A good alternative is to tell your child that they broke a rule, there will be consequences, but you need some time to think about what they will be. If you've really mastered the art of being firm and calm, you'll even be able to collaboratively come up with the consequences with your child.

Consistent consequences serve a purpose that is similar to predictable consequences. They leave less room for your child to feel surprised or bullied and they give your child the opportunity to make an informed decision about whether or not to engage in a behavior. Last time your child played for too long, she lost her privileges. This time, the same thing will happen. If you want to scale consequences (meaning making them more severe the more times a rule is broken), that's an option. Just make sure your child is aware of how the consequence will scale over time. No surprises, and no randomness based on how you're feeling or how much your child has upset you on that particular day. Also, make sure that the consequences you come up with are ones that you're willing to follow through on. Making empty threats that you don't follow through on is a great way to teach your child not to take you seriously.

Sometimes, you may decide that something needs to change in terms of the consequences for a given behavior. Again, just make sure that this is communicated with your child. It's perfectly acceptable to tell your child, "These consequences don't seem to be working. We need to try something different so we can help you stay motivated to follow your plan." Avoid shaming or making it sound like you want your child to feel pain or discomfort. Instead, you want to put loving but firm pressure on them to grow.

Finally, the consequences you give your child need to be relevant to the wrongdoing. If your child sneaks in an extra hour of gaming in the middle of the night, the consequence should be something that remedies the damage caused by that. For example, you may choose to remove your child's gaming system from his room (probably a good idea anyway), so that he sleeps through the night and doesn't have the temptation to play. Another consequence could be that he now has to play video games out in the common areas during his video game time so you can watch him and remind him when it's time to stop. This is a natural consequence of your child being dishonest and sneaking in video game time. He will experience what it's like to have trust lost.

You won't be able to come up with every consequence for every possible situation in the beginning, but it will be helpful to think of a few early on in the process. Remember that there is a difference between consequences and punishment. A consequence is a result, good or bad, of an action. A punishment is an unpleasant consequence meant to deter a certain behavior. Try to think of consequences that are more than just a simple punishment and are instead a remedy to a mistake that will teach your child something of value.

By having consequences that are predictable, consistent, and relevant, you increase your odds of cultivating a behavioral change in your child. Your child will most likely take advantage of any loopholes that are available, because that's what children (and many adults) do. Children do what works. If they discover that a sincere apology and some buttering-up will convince you to skip the consequences, they'll do it. In addition, your word will mean less and it will be that much more difficult to get them to take your boundaries seriously later on.

Stick to your rules. No matter what.

Chapter Six:
Executing the Plan

The reason I spent five chapters preparing you rather than just diving into the action is because this is not going to be an easy experience for you. Even if it goes smoothly, this is something that you've not done before. You may be feeling scared of confrontation, sad about having to upset your child, or even guilty for "letting" your child get to this point with video games. You may also be doubting whether or not your concerns are valid or whether you might be overreacting. This is all normal and to be expected. Reach out to your support network and then move forward with your plan one step at a time.

The Talk

Initiating

I've worked with lots of families over the years, and there is still no way to predict how a certain interaction will go. I can do my best as a mental health professional and communication coach to prepare you for the possible obstacles you'll face, but there is ultimately no script that will work in all situations. In order to stay in a place of calm authority throughout the talk, it's important that you have a confident understanding of what you're doing, why you're doing it, and how you're going to do it. If any part of this process doesn't make sense to you or feels inappropriate for your situation, take some time to revisit the earlier chapters or bounce your ideas off an advisor.

When it's time, sit down somewhere with your child and let them know you want to have a talk. While it may seem unimportant, make sure you physically position yourself in a way that is respectful and non-threatening. Don't gang up on your child by standing over her with your spouse while she sits on the floor playing video games. Sit around a table or somewhere equally comfortable, speak in a calm voice, and speak one at a time.

Keep your cool. If you notice yourself getting angry enough to want to raise your voice, stop the conversation and suggest everyone take a moment to step away and cool down. A time out is an incredibly useful tool when it comes to keeping the peace. Go to your separate corners, take some deep breaths, and revisit the topic later. It will be easier to keep your cool if you have a plan for how to deal with your child's potential objections and negative responses. It's expected that you may get a little frustrated and angry, but if it feels like it's getting out of your control, stop.

Remember that this is not a "this is what's happening because we're the parents and you're the child" type of conversation. There may be a need for that if your child is particularly resistant, but don't start there. At first, try to work collaboratively with your child. Ask her if she thinks her gaming is a problem. State your concerns and see what she thinks. If she disagrees, you can acknowledge her point of view without agreeing with it. You can say something like, "I hear what you're saying. I understand it's hard. We still have to do this because what's going on right now isn't healthy for you or for us."

Start the conversation by reminding your child that you aren't judging them and that you aren't doing this to try and hurt them. Remind him that you aren't doing your job as parents if you do nothing when he is doing something that you see as unhealthy. Afterwards, simply and calmly state what your goal is for your child. An example would be saying, "We're going to help you cut down on the amount of time you game. Right now, you play for about x hours per day. We are going to set a limit for x hours a day."

At this point, it's likely your child will be upset and have objections. It will be helpful to have written down a list of the negative consequences of your child's gaming. Perhaps his grades have gone down, he's spent less time with friends, or he's stopped engaging in hobbies he used to like. Calmly reflecting these consequences back to your child can be an effective way to increase his awareness of the problem, though you will still likely hear excuses. Remember to acknowledge that you hear your child when he objects. You can still respectfully disagree afterwards and remind him that this is part of your job as parents. Don't get too caught up arguing or splitting hairs with your child. This is especially apropos for teenagers; they are masters of lawyer-like arguing. If your child argues, listen and reflect back what they said. Express your disagreement simply and succinctly, then move on.

Once you've told your child what your goal is, express to him that you're open to hearing his thoughts about what would be a possible compromise or alternative goal. This is potentially a very powerful way to help your child feel empowered in this process. Any opportunity you have to show your child that you are open to hearing his thoughts and feelings will increase your odds of success. It has been supported in studies that a less confrontational approach is more likely to succeed in helping with addiction[viii]. This doesn't mean you have to obey whatever your child says, but it bears repeating that actively listening to and acknowledging your child goes a long way.

Asking Questions

Since we're on the topic of listening to your child, we may as well discuss my favorite technique for making sure people feel listened to: asking questions. Chances are, you've tried to ask your child some questions and they either haven't answered them, been dishonest, or only given brief answers. Learning how to ask questions in a way that elicits a response is a powerful tool that is helpful to everyone, not just parents. Again, there are no guarantees. Your child might be so guarded and insecure that she won't open up at all. If this is the case, it can be helpful to find your child a therapist or counselor that she feels comfortable talking to.

Asking questions is an art form. It's what I do for a living and I still struggle from time to time. Not only do we want to ask the right questions, but we want to ask them in the right way, with the right tone, and at the right time. For example, we don't want to ask questions that are too leading or closed-ended. A leading question is a question that is asked in such a way that it "fishes" for a certain response. An example of a leading question is, "You don't want to play video games for the rest of your life, do you?" That question is pushing for a specific answer. Stick with open-ended questions (questions that can't be answered with "yes" or "no") such as, "if you stopped playing video games, what would you be doing?" or, "what are some other things you think are interesting or fun?" Use your own wording depending on your personality and that of your child, but keep it respectful and genuine.

People are more willing to answer questions if they feel the asker is genuinely curious. Try not to ask these questions with the mindset of changing your child's behavior. Instead, become genuinely curious about your child and what is going on with him. Your child will sense that you are being sincere and it's likely to improve responses. If your child provides you with answers that you don't like, refrain from overt displays of judgment or disgust. There's no quicker way to shut someone down from wanting to talk than to scoff at their answers.

While this is best left to a therapist, it may be worth doing some research into the topic of motivational interviewing. I'm not going to get too into the technicalities of it here since it strays too far from the core message of this book. However, it can be a helpful topic to learn about if you want to try to increase motivation in your child[ix]. Again, this is a therapeutic technique that often takes many years of training to perfect. However, you can use some of the basic principles behind it to improve the odds of your child responding well to your questions. Here are the basic processes behind motivational interviewing[x].

    1.   Engaging: working collaboratively with your child.

Developing a relationship of trust in which your child feels comfortable with you and is willing to engage in the process.
   2. Focusing: directing the conversation gently to move towards discovering motivation. Keeping focused on the issue.
   3. Evoking: eliciting confidence and hope in your child and fostering your child's *own* motivation to change.
   4. Planning: collaboratively helping your child come up with a plan for change and committing to it.

How do you do these four things? To put it very simply, you approach your child in a non-judgmental, genuinely curious, collaborative way. As with any approach, there are no guarantees. I can, however, guarantee that you will get the same results if you keep doing the same thing, so try something different. The ultimate goal is to help your child discover her own motivation for change and collaboratively come up with a plan for how to tackle the problem. Your child is much more likely to follow through on her plan than your plan.

At the end of the day, the hard truth is that you are the parent and you're responsible for your child's health and well-being. If you've tried everything and nothing seems to be working, it's not wrong to exercise your authority, set limits, and enforce them yourself. The difference between most parents' natural inclination and my approach is that my approach uses this as a *last resort*. Being authoritative may work, but it is the approach most likely to lead to resentment, resistance, and arguments[xi]. Even if you have to be authoritative, avoid being *authoritarian*, which involves hostility, threats, and ruling with an iron fist. That may bring about short-term results, but it is not an ideal long-term plan. Authoritative simply means exercising your authority in a calm, confident manner.

Setting the Ground Rules

Once you've had the talk with your child, it's time to let them know what the plan is and how it's going to be carried out. The most important aspect of this phase is to explain things in a very matter-of-fact way without trying to incite fear or demonstrate dominance. You are explaining what your child needs to do and what she can expect to happen if those expectations aren't met. Your goal is to do it the same way you would explain the rules of a board game. Here's an example.

You: OK, so we've decided what's going to happen. For the next week, you've agreed to cut your video game time down from 8 hours a day to 4 hours a day. I know it's going to be difficult, but I believe you can do it. As long as you stick to these rules, we are going to pay for you to go to martial arts so you can still have fun and be with other people. We aren't doing this to punish you, we are doing it to help you be happier in the long run.

If you break these rules, we've decided what the consequences will be. If you go past your daily limit of video gaming, you lose your gaming privileges the entire next day and will need to find another way to spend your free time. If this happens three times, you will have the video game system taken out of your room and your phone taken away. If you continue to find ways to break the rules after that, you will continue to lose privileges, and we will decide each one when the time comes. Does that make sense and sound fair?

Remember to do your best to come from a place of love and genuine concern. I know this is probably occurring at a time when you're sick and tired of your child's habit, which is why there's an entire chapter on taking care of yourself before you even begin to embark on this process. You need to stay calm, consistent, firm, and loving. That is not an easy task, so engage in the level of self-care that you need in order to be successful.

For some of you, this will be very difficult. You may have been raised in such an authoritarian household that you go to the other extreme when parenting your children. Unfortunately, giving your children too much leeway can lead to them not knowing how to deal with any kind of limits or boundaries. I encourage you to think about the benefit that comes from having boundaries even though your experience with them was negative. Just setting boundaries is not a repeat of the bad stuff your parents did. You are going to break the cycle not by being overly permissive, but by being strict in the *right* way: with love, compassion, and calm assertiveness.

Dealing with Resistance

It's almost a guarantee that you will experience resistance from your child. Either they will make excuses for why their video gaming is not a problem, lie about their gaming habit, or they will become outright defiant and simply state they don't want to change anything. In these cases, it's helpful to have some responses in mind so it's less necessary for you to come up with them on the spot when tempers have flared and emotions are running high.

Excuses

An excuse is any argument that a problem is either justified or not that much of a problem. An example of the excuses you might hear from your child are:

- I don't play that much.
- It's the only thing I like to do.
- All my friends play just as much as/more than I do.
- It's how people have fun these days.
- I'm spending time with my friends.

The list could probably go on endlessly, but you get the picture. Your child will likely find some way to convince you to continue letting her play as often as she has been. She may try to convince you that your view of video games is the problem and that you shouldn't feel the way you do about her gaming habit.

Whenever your child makes an excuse, try to listen to what she is saying. Your natural inclination will probably be to say something that directly contradicts or invalidates what your child is saying. For example, if your child says, "All my friends are playing this much," you may feel the urge to launch into the old "if your friends jumped off a bridge" script. I have one word of advice if you want to go that route: don't.

Instead of arguing or invalidating your child, start by hearing her. Not just nodding, but actually listening and reflecting back what you heard. Here is an example of how you might respond to your child when she starts making excuses.

Child: I can't stop playing. This is how I spend time with my friends!

You: It sounds like you really like spending time with your friends this way. I bet it would be hard to lose that. How can we make sure you still get to spend a lot of time with your friends even if you're spending less time gaming?

Child: There isn't any way.

You: So, video games are the only way to spend time with friends? Do any of your friends do anything other than play video games?

Child: Yeah.

You: So I know you can, too. Let's talk about other things you might like to do instead to spend time with your friends. You don't have to stop playing games completely, but it will be healthier for you to do some other things, too. I know it's hard to stop something that is so fun, but it really has caused some problems and we need to find a way to help you avoid having even more problems because of it.

Obviously, this dialogue will shift depending on the age of your child, your child's response, and many other factors. This is one of countless different conversations that could potentially happen. The point of this example is not to be a script that you follow word-for-word, but an illustration of the manner in which you should focus on speaking to your child.

Notice that all the responses are respectful, demonstrate that the parent is listening, and provide an offer to work collaboratively with the child. In addition, the child is ultimately not being given a choice when it comes to whether or not she will play fewer video games. You are not relinquishing your power as a parent. You are maintaining your power while simultaneously empowering your child to play an active role in her own recovery.

If you are going to "lay down the law," it's going to go a long way to give your child some control in some areas so it doesn't feel like they are being completely controlled. The more children feel controlled, the more they will try to exert control themselves in other areas of their lives. This can come in the form of aggression, rebellion, and disrespect.

Defiance

If your child isn't the arguing type, he may simply try to defy the rules and get away with it. For example, your child may wait until you go to sleep so that he can get up and play video games without you knowing. This can be an incredibly frustrating experience, and the natural reaction may be to show your child how angry you are and how unacceptable that action is. As you can probably guess by now, that isn't the ideal way to approach it.

Think back to our discussions about consequences. Using that information, how would you respond to catching your child trying to outright defy your rules? The ideal approach would be calm, loving, firm boundaries that are clear and non-reactive. Try to avoid an impulsive response such as saying, "That's it! No more PlayStation in your room if we can't trust you!" Remember, if you're so heated that you feel the urge to yell at or punish your child, you can say something along the lines of, "This is not OK. There will be consequences for this and I'll let you know when I figure out what they are." Then, go cool down and think about what the response needs to be. In most situations, it won't be an emergency you need to respond to immediately. Taking the time to practice your new skills will increase the odds of the following interactions being productive rather than destructive. Here's how a conversation might go.

You: It's not OK that you were playing games when we decided you shouldn't be. What consequence do you think you earned?

Child: None.

You: I understand you don't want consequences, but you knew what you were doing was wrong, and we talked about how breaking rules will lead to consequences every time.

Child: I can't play for five minutes.

You: That's better than nothing, but that's a very small consequence, and being dishonest is breaking a very important rule. We have decided that you can't play any games tomorrow. In the future, if you play video games when you know you're not supposed to, you will no longer be able to keep your PlayStation in your room. Does that seem fair?

Child: No!

You: I know it sounds hard, but we need you to understand that it is never OK to lie or be dishonest to us. You will get your games back the day after tomorrow and we will trust you to play only when you are allowed. If you follow the rules, you will earn our trust back and you can keep the PlayStation in your room. It's up to you.

Once again, the dialogue may go very different than what is written here. The purpose of these examples is to highlight the general attitude that you should try to adopt. There isn't any judgment, criticism, or attempts to be mean. Instead, there is respectful dialogue (even when the child is angry and being unreasonable). The child is given opportunities to take part in his consequences. If he refuses to play by the rules, it is pointed out that he is making a choice to give his power back to his parents.

Notice that the parent is still listening to the child and reflecting back what the child is saying. However, they are not agreeing with the child or giving in to the child's unreasonable attempts at bargaining. You need to maintain your power and control as a parent while also allowing your child some say in the matter. It's a delicate balance to find, but you will find it if you continue to practice. These skills do not only apply to video games; they apply to all behaviors, so practice when you can.

If Things Get Heated

I want to be crystal clear on this: if your child becomes physically aggressive and is old enough to comprehend what he's doing, it is OK to call the police. Keeping in line with the message of this book, children of all ages (and adults) need consequences in order to grow. If your child resorts to violence and isn't held accountable, nothing will magically change on its own and your child could end up being abusive in situations that are bound to cause him much more serious problems. The following link provides some good advice for parents who are dealing with abusive children: https://www.empoweringparents.com/article/is-it-time-to-call-the-police-on-your-child-assaultive-behavior-verbal-or-physical-abuse-drugs-and-crime/.

Most likely, your child will resort to verbal aggression or physical aggression towards inanimate objects like a pillow or the wall. This is still not OK and needs to be met with consequences as soon as possible. In these situations, it is very important not to impose consequences *during* the episode of aggression or intense anger. That will just be seen as engaging in the fight. Instead, keep yourself calm, remove yourself from the situation if necessary, and de-escalate the situation or allow it to de-escalate on its own.

De-escalating a situation basically means to calm everyone down and return the conversation to a place of calm civility. It is yet another art form that takes practice. Sometimes, the best you can do when a situation has become verbally aggressive is to remove yourself from it. Bear in mind, however, that simply walking away can also be seen as an act of aggression. If you've ever walked away from an angry person (or been walked away from), you understand that it is a very provocative act. While you may intend to do the right thing, it is often seen as a rejection and can cause the angry person to become more aggressive.

Removing yourself from a situation needs to be done calmly and methodically (are you seeing a pattern yet?). Let the person know you want to hear them, but currently can't because things have gotten too heated. Then, let them know that you want to return to the topic at a later time. Sometimes, it can be helpful to set up a specific time to revisit the conversation. For example, you could say, "we're both too angry to have a constructive conversation right now. I need a break, but I do want to hear what you have to say. I'm going to go cool down for a while and then we can talk about this again. How about we start this conversation again in an hour?"

Obviously, this is easier said than done. It's very challenging to speak in a calm and measured way when you are angry. This is why it's far better to do it early. The moment you notice a conversation getting more heated, it's a good idea to call for a little break. It's really difficult to do this successfully in the middle of a shouting match. Practicing mindfulness is a great way to get better at regulating your emotions before they get out of hand. To learn more, simply search for "mindfulness meditation" on Google. UCLA has a website that provides free audio files of guided mindfulness meditations. Visit **marc.ucla.edu/audio** to download some and try them out. These are best done preventatively, meaning before you get angry or enter a challenging situation.

Getting Technological Assistance

There are technologies and services available to help you control your child's use of electronics. It would take another book to go into all the options, so I'll lay out a few examples for you here. For instance, most video game consoles have parental control settings. Unfortunately, most children are savvy enough to get around these controls if they really want to, which is why they are intended to be supplemental tools rather than a complete solution to the problem. Consult the instruction manual or the company website to learn how to turn on parental controls for your child's specific gaming system.

Another service that is available is called OpenDNS (www.opendns.com). This is a service that you can utilize through your router to prevent certain websites from being viewed and even set time limits on certain devices in the house. Again, this is not 100% effective. You still need to monitor your child and build a trusting relationship with him so that the urge to defy the rules is minimized.

If your child primarily games on smartphones, there are unfortunately fewer ways to keep things under your control. If your child is addicted to his smartphone, sometimes the only answer is the dreaded flip phone, which has no functions other than calling and painfully slow texting. You can try asking your child to self-monitor how much time he spends using his phone, but I highly doubt that he will be able to do that successfully, especially since most adults can't.

An option with cell phones is to turn off your child's data capabilities so they can't play certain games outside of the house Wi-Fi. This will need to be coupled with close supervision and/or a service like OpenDNS that allows you to control traffic on your home network. As with most measures, this can easily be circumvented, but it's still better than nothing.

Monitoring is often a better alternative to controlling. There are tools available that allow you to monitor the internet activity at your home or the cell phone activity of everyone on your plan. Monitoring is superior to control in that it lets you know what's going on so you can respond accordingly. If the technology is setting the limits, that keeps you more separated from the process than you ideally should be.

Some options for monitoring include various apps like Mobicip (for Android, iOS, and Windows), Nischint (Android and iOS), and Watchover (iOS). By the time you read this, it's very possible that new services and apps have come out. A quick search for "monitor online activity app" will find you what you're looking for. It may take some trial and error before you discover the app that is best for you and your situation.

Withdrawal

You may wonder how it's possible for anyone to go through withdrawal from something that doesn't physically enter the body. It's important to differentiate between an emotional/mental withdrawal and a physical withdrawal. No, your child will likely not get the shakes or cold sweats as a result of quitting or cutting back on video games. They will, however, start to miss the stimulation and their brains will need to adjust to the lower levels of dopamine.

This makes sense if you think back on your personal experiences. Have you ever been on a vacation and then gone back to work the day you return? Doesn't it feel strange? Sometimes even depressing? Of course it does. Your mind is used to a certain kind of stimulation and can't simply switch back to normal when it all ends. If you spend a two-week vacation water skiing and skydiving, you're going to need to re-adjust to a slower, less intense lifestyle when you're done. It's just how our brains work. Try to think of your child as someone who has been skydiving for 12 hours a day every day. Stopping is going to be rough and may require a little patience on everyone's part.

Withdrawal from behavioral addictions has some similarities to withdrawal from substance addictions. For instance, it's very common for people to become irritable when they are no longer getting the stimulation they used to get from their addiction. As you might be able to imagine, being under-stimulated and frustrated on a consistent basis makes it hard to be calm and patient with others. You may have to cut your child a little slack during this period if she is grumpier than usual. This does not mean you need to tolerate abuse, however.

Because we aren't talking about chemicals, there's no way to really predict how long the withdrawal phase will last. Some children may need a few days while some may need a month or more. There's no real literature on video game withdrawal, so I can only go by what I've seen myself. Withdrawal, like any uncomfortable experience, can be made more comfortable if your child has ample opportunity to engage in other fun and interesting activities. If your child replaces playing video games with sitting in his room and feeling sorry for himself, then withdrawal is going to hit a bit harder for him. Make sure you encourage your child to have fun and spend time with friends in the days and weeks after making a change to his gaming habits.

Chapter Seven: Long-Term Challenges

While the initial talk and setting of ground rules may seem like it would be the most difficult part of this process, I don't think it is. It may be the most dramatic and scary, but the hardest part is staying consistent over the long-term and sticking to the plan one day at a time. You may get lucky and your child may adjust relatively quickly to the new rules, in which case, congratulations! However, chances are there will be a period of time where your child tries to push your boundaries and go back into old habits.

Remember that video gaming addiction shares many of the same qualities as drug or alcohol addiction. When your child goes through particularly stressful times or times of low structure (e.g. summer vacation) he will likely be drawn back into the soothing world of gaming. There may be a resurgence in excuses, attempts to manipulate, or outright defiance of the rules. When this happens, your approach needs to be exactly the same as before: calm, firm, assertive, and loving.

Rather than being critical, look at your child's desire to start playing more video games as a sign that she is in need of something. Perhaps she needs more social interaction, more recreational time, or perhaps she is struggling with anxiety, depression, or stress. One of the positive outcomes of lessening or removing an addictive behavior is that you get more insight into the problems that were causing the addictive behavior in the first place. For instance, your child may not have realized that her social interactions at school are causing her a lot of stress because she was numbing and escaping with video games. Now, she may be more aware of it and able to talk about it since it isn't being masked by a highly rewarding behavior.

Vacation and Special Occasions

Depending on your particular child, it may be perfectly fine to allow your child to play extra video games during a break or vacation. However, there should still be clearly-communicated boundaries and expectations. If you let her game without any accountability, it will be that much more difficult to rein it back in when she needs to return to school, work, or both. Alternatively, vacations may be one of the best opportunities to get your child into an activity that will take her mind off of video games and possibly ignite a passion for something else.

Some children will not do well with exceptions during vacations or special occasions. As with any addiction, a little exposure may end up being too much. This is particularly true if you have determined that your child needs to be completely off of video games. If this is the case, then allowing her to play video games during a school break will likely lead to problems. The chance of a smooth transition back to zero video gaming is slim to none.

This decision is ultimately up to you. If you've been closely monitoring your child and seeing how they're adjusting to life with fewer (or no) video games, then you should have a pretty good idea of how they'll react if given the opportunity to play more. More likely than not, a child who you've decided to take the moderation approach with will probably do better with vacations than a child who needs an abstinence-based approach.

Underlying Issues

I've touched on this a bit already, but it's worth repeating as often as possible. Anyone who becomes addicted to something is likely also struggling with underlying issues that are causing them to seek out an excessive amount of pleasure. Children who are very resilient, emotionally intelligent, and self-confident are much less likely to have an issue with any kind of addiction than children who are anxious, socially awkward, sensitive, or stressed out[xiii].

While it's helpful to do what I've outlined in this book, it may not be enough on its own. If underlying issues are severe enough, it's very common for addictions to simply morph rather than go away. For instance, drug addicts will often become addicted to food or sex when they initially get clean. This is due to the fact that the addiction is usually a symptom of a larger problem, and if the problem isn't dealt with, the addiction will simply shift to a new focus.

If it's available, I highly suggest getting your child into therapy during this process. He may be reluctant, but if you shop around, you're likely to find a therapist who has mastered the art of getting children to buy into the therapeutic process. As with everything in this world, there are no guarantees, but having someone safe to talk to about his problems may give your child a much-needed advantage during this challenging process.

Jenna's Story

Jenna was 20 years old when she first came into my office. Her parents referred her to therapy saying that she had been struggling with bouts of hopelessness and anxiety. Recently, Jenna's emotional issues had escalated to the point where she was engaging in cutting. Jenna spent the vast majority of her day playing video games and was unmotivated to attend school or find a job. She acknowledged that video games were her favorite way of coping with stress. She said it brought her a lot of relief from her anxiety.

Having done a thorough assessment on Jenna, I knew right off the bat that she was struggling with a lot more than video game addiction. I discovered that Jenna's parents got divorced when she was just eight years old. It was a nasty divorce and her parents were so busy fighting each other that they never processed what was happening with Jenna. Around the same time, Jenna had also experienced a very frightening car crash in which her mother was injured and almost died. When her mother came back from the hospital, she told Jenna everything was OK, but never really talked to her about her feelings.

Jenna had a rough combination of grief, loss, and unresolved trauma. If her parents had simply told her to stop playing video games, it's very likely that she would have discovered some other way to cope with the pain that she was harboring as a result of these events. She may have turned to drugs, became aggressive, or engaged in any number of other impulsive and self-destructive behaviors.

Jenna and I spent over a year talking about her parent's divorce, the car crash, and a lot of other life stressors. Slowly but surely, Jenna started to play fewer video games and stopped self-harming. She still played, but was now able to hold a job (two, in fact) and was spending more time with friends. In addition, she discovered she really enjoyed rock climbing, which became her new passion.

Jenna's story is a prime example of why just addressing video game use is sometimes insufficient. There are many factors that drive our behavior, and sometimes those factors are too complicated to deal with without professional help. This isn't to say that you're a bad parent if you can't "fix" your child on your own. It's just darn near impossible for *any* parent to act as a therapist for their child. As parents, we are far too emotionally invested in our children and are unable to be as objective as necessary to engage in the therapeutic process. It's the same reason surgeons won't operate on their own children. Even trained therapists send their children to outside professionals for help when necessary.

Is This Forever?

The idea of embarking on a process like this may seem completely exhausting, and that's understandable. It's likely you're wondering how long you're going to have to do this hard work. The truth is that there's no easy answer to that question. Your child may grow used to the new set of rules very quickly, in which case there's not much more you need to do other than enforce the rules on the rare occasion that your child tries to break them.

Some children will not adjust nearly as quickly, and this may be a longer process. For these situations, I can only reiterate how important it is to engage in regular self-care. I know I've mentioned it a hundred times already, but it can't be said enough. Being inconsistent in this process can undo a lot of progress very quickly. If you find yourself getting burned out, make a note of it and do something about it before you throw your hands up in the air and surrender to the way things were.

Even if you have a child that requires regular rule reinforcement, chances are you will still be able to take a more passive role as things move forward. It's not human nature for children to continue fighting the same rules over and over unless they have a reason to believe they can win. This is why consistency and not budging is so important. Your child will adjust to the new rules much more quickly if he is certain that there is no way he's going to change them through whining, manipulation, or any other method. If, on the other hand, your child has evidence to show that enough pushing will work, it may take much longer for the rule-enforcing phase to come to a close.

Depending on how old your child is, this whole process may be very short. If your child is planning on moving out of the home soon, for instance, you are clearly not going to be able to enforce these rules anymore. At that point, your child's life is in his hands and your level of influence will drop dramatically. Some parents may try to continue enforcing limits after their children leave the house. This usually doesn't go well and is not something I recommend. If your child is out in the world and is not functioning the way they need to, they will experience the consequences of that, and that is a good thing.

One of the biggest disservices you can do for your child is to shield them from the real-world consequences of their actions. I often see parents very openly state that they will allow their children to move back in with them if they don't succeed. While there are certainly some situations in which this is appropriate, it is generally a bad message to send to a child. Our job as parents is to teach our children how to have successful lives without our help. If we always offer a safety net or are willing to bail them out of every tough situation, we're teaching them that they are not ultimately responsible for the choices they make and the actions they take, and that message can lead to a lifetime of irresponsible and immature behavior.

Epilogue

Congratulations on being willing to look at a very challenging issue. It would probably be more comfortable to simply let things continue the way they are and hope that things spontaneously get better. Instead, you've taken proactive steps and decided to try something new so that your family can have a better life. I have tremendous respect for you and hope that you are giving yourself credit for the effort you've put into this process.

Video game addiction is a complicated issue with a lot of contributing factors. I hope that this book has given you some helpful guidance towards successfully addressing your child's excessive use of video games. As a parent myself, I understand how frustrating and scary it can be to see your child engaged in self-destructive behavior that *seems* like it could be stopped with a simple decision.

If you've learned nothing else in this book, I hope you take with you a few key concepts.

1. Plan – Before taking direct action, think about your child's gaming habit and decide the best course of action. Decide how you're going to talk to him, what rules you're going to set, and how you're going to respond to fighting and resistance.
2. Determine your attitude – Commit to adopting an attitude of loving but firm authority. The boundaries that you set will likely feel like punishments to your child. This is especially true if you are hostile, cold, or aggressive.
3. Be consistent and predictable – If you have a rule, enforce it every time. Being consistent gives your child the opportunity to make fully informed choices about how to behave. If your child *knows* that playing more than x hours a day will result in the loss of his game console, she knows exactly what to expect when she crosses that line.

These three principles by themselves can make a huge difference in how effective any discipline is. Of course you aren't going to be perfect. You may slip up here and there. Forgive yourself and recommit to the process. An occasional slip may prolong the process a bit, but that is no reason to give up. Stick with it and it will pay off.

As a self-published author, I truly appreciate the fact that you've taken the time to purchase and read my book. If you wish to contact me, I am available through email at **jeffmft@gmail.com**. You can also visit my website at **www.practicallysane.net**, where I host a blog and a newsletter sign-up for anyone who wants to be notified about my latest work. If you like this book, please take the time to leave an honest review on its Amazon page.

Thank you, and good luck on your journey!

[i]Notes

Muraven, M., & Baumeister, R. F. (2000). Self-regulation and depletion of limited resources: Does self-control resemble a muscle?. *Psychological bulletin, 126*(2), 247.

[ii] Powell, K. (2006). Neurodevelopment: how does the teenage brain work?. *Nature, 442*, 865-867.

[iii] Perkins Jr, C. C., & Cacioppo, A. J. (1950). The effect of intermittent reinforcement on the change in extinction rate following successive reconditionings. *Journal of Experimental Psychology, 40*(6), 794.

[iv] Kent, S. L. (2010). *The Ultimate History of Video Games: from Pong to Pokemon and beyond... the story behind the craze that touched our lives and changed the world.* Three Rivers Press.

[v] Kuss, D. J. (2013). Internet gaming addiction: current perspectives. *Psychology research and behavior management, 6*, 125.

[vi] King, D. L., & Delfabbro, P. H. (2014). Is preoccupation an oversimplification? A call to examine cognitive factors underlying internet gaming disorder. *Addiction, 109*(9), 1566-1567.

[vii] Stall, R., & Biernacki, P. (1986). Spontaneous remission from the problematic use of substances: An inductive model derived from a comparative analysis of the alcohol, opiate, tobacco, and food/obesity literatures. *International Journal of the Addictions, 21*(1), 1-23.

[viii] Miller, W. R., Benefield, R. G., & Tonigan, J. S. (1993). Enhancing motivation for change in problem drinking: a controlled comparison of two therapist styles. *Journal of consulting and clinical psychology, 61*(3), 455.

[ix] Lundahl, B. W., Kunz, C., Brownell, C., Tollefson, D., & Burke, B. L. (2010). A meta-analysis of motivational interviewing: Twenty-five years of empirical studies. *Research on social work practice, 20*(2), 137-160.

[x] Miller, W. R., & Rollnick, S. (2012). *Motivational interviewing: Helping people change.* Guilford press.

[xi] Joseph, M. V., & John, J. (2008). Impact of parenting styles on child development. *Global Academic Society Journal: Social Science Insight, 1*(5), 16-25.

[xii] Benard, B. (1991). Fostering resiliency in kids: Protective factors in the family, school, and community.